100 IDEAS
FOR TEACHING
GEOGRAPHY

Andy Leeder

continuum
LONDON • NEW YORK

Continuum International Publishing Group

The Tower Building   80 Maiden Lane
11 York Road   Suite 704
London   New York
SE1 7NX   NY 10038

www.continuumbooks.com

British Library Cataloguing-in-Publication Data
A catalogue record for this book is available from the British Library.

ISBN: 0–8264–8538–3 (paperback)

Library of Congress Cataloging-in-Publication Data
A catalog record for this book is available from the Library of Congress.

Typeset by Ben Cracknell Studios
Printed and bound in Great Britain by MPG Books Ltd, Bodmin, Cornwall

CONTENTS

SECTION 4 The classroom environment

SECTION 5 Field trips

SECTION 9 Homework and revision

SECTION 10 Information and communications technology

SECTION 11 **Other key ideas**

This book has been written with a view to helping geographers new to the teaching profession and to encourage experienced geographers to further develop their teaching and learning strategies. The tips contained in the book are tried and tested and are the result of over twenty-five years of experience in the classroom. I am indebted to my colleagues, who have been central to developing many of the ideas; their inspiration and commitment to helping students and to flying the flag for geography have been great motivating factors in writing this book. When you witness something that works well and moves students on, it should be recognized. Moreover, as the subject has developed at a rapid pace over the years, not least in the resources available to enhance learning in the subject, it is important to signal the new opportunities that are at hand.

The main focus of the book is to promote the notion that learning programmes can be varied, fun and challenging. Given the competition that geography faces in a crowded and developing curriculum, the book also suggests strategies to help maintain its rightful position as an essential subject for study beyond Key Stage 3. Dip into the ideas and tips given here, and develop them to suit your own needs and circumstances. Take risks in your own teaching and always be prepared to learn from others. Happy reading.

A special mention needs to be made of Graham Heywood, Alan Moon, Gererd Dixie and Steve Brenchley. All of them are exceptional teachers in their own right and great ambassadors for the subject.

The cartoons used in the book were drawn by Roy Fitzsimmonds.

GETTING THE MOST FROM THIS BOOK

Maintaining a high profile for the subject

If the management team in your school is devoid of geographers and if they retain some of their former prejudices about the subject (it's all about colouring maps and finding out about places like Ceylon – yes, I know it's called Sri Lanka now!), you need to take action. Particularly in the post- 'Opportunities and Excellence' era, in which schools have a responsibility to develop, widen and update their post-14 curriculum, complacent geographers will lose out, and so will the students. What can you do?

o Make managers sit up and take notice by achieving consistently good exam results. Residuals scores will confirm that you can get the best out of the full ability range. If you join a school where the starting point in geography is problematic, work hard to get the teaching and learning strategies right.

o Think carefully about your strategy throughout Key Stage 3 and in particular the experience that students have just ahead of Year 9 options. If there is no structured, whole-school approach to option choices, ensure that time is given over in lessons to explain the rich pathways for geographers beyond 16.

o Remind managers constantly about their responsibilities to ensure education for citizenship and sustainable futures. Illustrate how geographers can take the lead.

o Remind them of the kudos with parents which stems from successful school trips.

o Overtly illustrate the way that geography contributes to their literacy, numeracy and ICT strategy.

As with Idea 1, you need to keep parents informed about the many valid reasons for studying geography beyond 14 and into post-16 education. If your teaching and learning strategies are sound and secure, the students should support you in your drive to keep geography buoyant post-14. However, parents, like senior managers, have their own prejudices about the subject.

o Use opportunities such as open evenings to present the subject in a stimulating way (see Idea 3).
o Whatever the format for Year 9 and Year 11 'choices/options' evenings, ensure that you have well-presented flyers to illustrate career paths and pathways.
o Challenge the parents with information about how their son or daughter is going to be knowledgeable and ready to play a full part in our fast-changing world.
o Make them aware of the fact that geography has moved on. Don't hold back from using and applying information and communications technology (ICT) to a range of geography contexts. Educate them that geography is also about reasoned opinions, challenge, and values and attitudes.

Open evenings are a great opportunity to show prospective students and their parents just what a stimulating and challenging subject geography is. Whether it is an open evening targeted at children transferring from primary schools or perhaps an evening set up to recruit prospective A-level students, it is worth making the display and/or activities dynamic.

Display work produced by students at all different levels. Ensure that the work on display is assessed. If a grading or level system is used, ensure that both the students and their parents understand the criteria for assessment. Of equal importance, make sure that teacher comments are formative and that appropriate praise is given. Areas for further development should be suggested, clearly indicating that the department has challenge and development at the heart of its work.

Alongside students' work, display the rich array of teaching resources used in the department. From selected pages in textbooks to worksheets and photographs, challenge the visitors by highlighting how and why the material is used. To avoid the more sterile displays seen at too many open evenings, try to introduce some 'hands-on' activities:

o accessing CD-ROMs or the school's intranet;
o quizzes, or 'where in the world' picture challenges.

A dramatic impact can be made by constructing a tropical rainforest room. Use loads of heaters and tea urns to generate heat and humidity, borrow lots of luxurious plants and set up a large screen showing video clips of the fantastic ecosystem, combined with dramatic images of damaging exploitation.

Geographical issues are rarely out of the news. When a major event occurs, such as the Asian tsunami of December 2004, or the flooding at Boscastle in August 2004, even the tabloid newspapers dedicate several column inches to the event. Despite extensive parallel coverage on television and radio, some students appear to know very little about the event, apart from the headline. A small minority remain blissfully ignorant of it.

If you are lucky enough to have a central display area, why not dedicate the space to the theme of 'Geography in the News'? A determined effort to keep the display up to date will keep the students interested and expectant. If the presentational style is carefully considered and accessible to students, it will engage them and may encourage them to find out more. It will give them access to events or news items that may be of huge significance, but may be reported only in some of the more environmentally aware newspapers such as the *Guardian* or the *Independent*.

Have a world map as the permanent backdrop to the display to increase knowledge of location. Have a large banner headline to draw them in. Display cuttings and photographs from the original article but prepare a 'key facts' summary. Prepare a few searching questions to stimulate further thinking.

The good news is that the teaching staff do not have to get involved in changing the display on a regular basis. Once staff have invested the time to get the display backdrop in place, subsequent work can be handed over to a student who has been identified as having exceptional gifts and talents (see Idea 98) or to a willing A-level student. The end product is educative and inclusive, and helps the geography department to cement its profile within the school.

ASSEMBLIES 1: FINITE RESOURCES

From time to time, geography teachers are asked to plan and deliver the whole-school assembly. Look at this as an opportunity rather than a chore. It's the perfect opportunity to raise the profile of the subject. It could also be a good opportunity to deliver one of the elements of citizenship assigned to the geography team. This tip suggests an assembly which can be delivered by one member of the geography team; the next tip requires the involvement of a small number of 'volunteer' students.

SPACESHIP EARTH: FINITE RESOURCES
This assembly will be significantly enhanced if the delivery is supported by a few carefully selected images. Ideally, they would be projected from a laptop, but overhead transparencies would suffice. Launch the assembly by talking about unnecessary waste around the school (paper/electric lights/running taps, etc.). Move on to the obvious financial implications of waste, but quickly move on further to the wider issue of using up finite resources. Students quickly grasp the message if you portray the Earth as a spaceship. Within the spaceship an array of cupboards contain a wealth of resources. After continuous raiding, the cupboards will eventually be bare. Pose the question, what can we all do to prevent us getting to this point?

Another idea for an assembly is to alert students to the fact that, in life, differences of opinion exist across a multitude of issues. Moreover, when difficult decisions need to be made, compromise may not be an option; some people may be unhappy with the outcome.

Start by focusing minds on a school-based issue on which differences of opinion exist. One example includes the controversy of having an 'open school' policy throughout lunchtime, as opposed to a 'lock out'. Alternatively, there are often disputes simmering when changes to the school uniform are being considered. Whatever is chosen, selected students could voice a range of strong opinions to the audience. The teacher in charge of the assembly could reflect on each opinion and debate the potential for compromise. He or she might point out that compromise could be the worst of all options. An extension to this theme would be to introduce the notion of appeasement for those who ultimately feel let down.

Having focused minds, move swiftly on to parallel geography debates. Repeat the mode of delivery using the students.

○ Perhaps the issue is local: alternative routes for a bypass?
○ Perhaps it's national: airport expansion on the back of ever-increasing numbers of budget airlines?
○ Perhaps it's international: aid or trade for development in Africa?

Differences of opinion? Hard decisions? Possibility of compromise? Appeasement? All are features of a geographical debate, ripe for assemblies.

ASSEMBLIES 2: DIFFICULT DECISIONS, LOTS OF OPINIONS

The world of work is constantly changing, and change occurs at an ever-increasing rate. This idea urges all geographers to maintain an interest in and a determined effort to keep up to date with the pathways and careers open to students who study geography. In a curriculum that becomes ever more competitive, particularly in Key Stages 4 and 5, we need to remind students and their parents of the opportunities that lie beyond study in school.

While we know that geography develops a wide range of transferable skills attractive to employers, it is necessary for students and parents to be informed of this. Help is at hand: you do not have to reinvent the wheel! The Royal Geographical Society (in association with the Institute of British Geographers), can provide you with a wealth of material for use in your school. From free posters to a free Microsoft PowerPoint presentation, a free video (why choose geography at GCSE?) and interviews with well-known personalities, they can supply you with all you need. Go to their website at www.rgs.org and follow the links through 'education' and then 'advice and careers' for all you need.

As was stated in Idea 1, geography can be a key subject in delivering essential skills and cross-curricular themes. There are times, however, when students and parents ask us what is unique about the subject that will provide students with something that others cannot provide. Always have at your fingertips a response. The list below may give you a starting point. Geography allows students:

○ to answer questions about the natural and human worlds, using different scales of inquiry to view them from different perspectives;
○ to develop awareness and understanding of a range of peoples and cultures, and a respect for many different attitudes, views and beliefs;
○ to gain experiences that help them make connections between themselves, their communities and the wider world;
○ to explore issues of environmental change and sustainable development, and develop the skills and attitudes necessary for active involvement as citizens;
○ to develop and extend their investigative and problem-solving skills, including skills in number and information and communications technology (ICT), inside and outside the classroom;
○ to recognize the need for a just and equitable society, and their own role in making this possible.

Lesson activities: starters

GET YOUR STUDENTS WARMED UP!

This idea will explain some of the reasons why educationalists promote the idea of 'mental warm-ups' and kinaesthetic activity, both of which can form the basis of any starter activity.

There is a wide range of research to confirm that a 'warmed-up' brain makes for more effective learning. Warm-ups, particularly the use of more ambitious warm-up exercises that might require movement or sorting or grouping, etc., may be of particular value to students who have special needs. There is a wealth of information on the advantages of using a wide variety of learning styles, not least because we know that students learn effectively in very different ways and in a multitude of ways.

Geography provides a rich context for devising starter activities. As the National Learning Strategy makes clear, the teacher who recognizes the value of shaping the learning programme around a combination of visual, auditory, kinaesthetic and collaborative experiences is a teacher who will access the full range of students' learning strengths.

Access to learning through visual stimulus alone illustrates the head start that geography teachers have, compared to others. Without stopping to think why, we enthusiastically embrace the use of photographs, diagrams, sketches, film, video, cartoons, maps, etc. You will see from the examples in Ideas 11–16 that visual stimuli can form the basis for many starter activities. They engage students and draw them into the rest of the learning programme. More often than not, they are fun. It may be that starter activities are the place where geographers who up until now have relied on a very conservative range for their learning programme decide to experiment. The dividends will be for all to see and enjoy.

Beyond the 'learning rationale' (see Idea 9), you should recognize the value of using starter activities to ensure a purposeful and crisp start to the lesson. In reality, teachers will always face situations where students trickle in from different locations around the school. From time to time, small groups within the class may be held back for a few minutes, perhaps after an assembly or by their form tutor following registration. Starter activities can be effective time-fillers. Their use sends a clear message to the students that the lesson will be purposeful from the outset, no matter what the delay. Students can be engaged while lesson resources are being distributed. This is particularly important in geography classes, as geography teachers often use a multiplicity of stimulus materials such as photographs, maps, worksheets, texts, all in the same lesson.

Starter activities can be the chosen way to link back to the work undertaken in a previous lesson; teachers know the advantages of a seamless transition from one lesson to the next. Starters can serve as the reinforcement of previously learned knowledge. They can be an avenue to greater understanding; they can be set up to further develop a previously learned skill. The starter can serve to engage and draw in a student who has missed the previous lesson.

Before you review the exemplar activities (Ideas 11–16), perhaps a word of warning is appropriate. Starter activities work best when they are used habitually. Students will accept that each lesson begins this way. If the starter activity is apparent when students enter the room, the teacher may not need to explain what is required. A second word of warning: don't allow the starter activity to last the entire lesson!

A CRISP START TO THE LESSON

AMAZING FACTS

As the students arrive, display (in any format) a sequence of facts about any given country. Students need to make an educated guess as to what country the information relates. When the cohort has arrived and the last few students have had a chance to absorb the facts, ask the students for their views; ask them why they have come to this conclusion. A subtle development is for you to deliberately insert one false fact. If you do this, students need to state which is the false fact and why they think that it is likely to be untrue for the country concerned. The activity is easily differentiated.

You do not have to spend hours researching amazing facts for a range of countries; an Internet search will provide you with all you need. Effective search words in Google seem to be 'Amazing facts about . . .'.

Before you move to the next tip, identify the country and identify the false clue!

o It's the sixth largest country in the world.
o Chess was invented here.
o Bison used to roam the central plains of this country.
o It has the highest cricket ground in the world (2,444 metres above sea level).
o Its railway system is the biggest employer in the world.
o Until 1896, it was the only supplier of diamonds to the world.
o It is the world's largest democracy.

A starter activity that makes use of a slide show is ideal when you are about to start a new topic and you want students to gain a 'sense of place'. This is particularly important when the location to be studied is unfamiliar (e.g. the Caatinga drought zone of north-eastern Brazil).

To ensure that the activity is effective, the classroom should be set up with a computer and projector. Staff will need to have a basic competence in using Microsoft PowerPoint.

The name of the new location need not be given to students in the first instance. Ask them to watch a sequence of slides which build up and create an understanding of life in the new location. Depending on the purpose behind the study, slides showing both a physical dimension and a human dimension are ideal.

For the Caatinga drought zone, among the slides you might use are pictures showing:

o a dried-up river bed;
o a blazing sun;
o malnourished people;
o poor rural houses;
o a failed harvest.

Experience shows that a five-second delay between each slide is effective, and a maximum of 20 slides should be used. Depending on how competent staff are in setting up the slide show, student attention is enhanced by using a limited range of entry and exit sequences in the PowerPoint. The final two slides can include thumbnails of all of the slides used. Running the sequence twice is worthwhile.

The lesson can continue by asking students what they know about the place. The level of sophistication in the selected slides makes this starter appropriate for students across all key stages and up to A level.

WHERE IN THE WORLD?

'Where in the world' is a good starter activity to use when you want to develop the students' knowledge of location. Provide your students with a number of coloured photographs and perhaps a climate graph (unnamed). Alternatively, you could set the pictures up as a recurring slide-show sequence through your laptop and projector.

Students study the pictures and are asked to suggest where in the world the case study or focus area is likely to be. As more of these starter activities are used, students will become aware of the questions to ask themselves as they study the pictures. Initially, students might need help in these organizing questions – prompts such as:

o Does architectural style suggest anything?
o Does the physical landscape give any clues?
o Is the vegetation type helpful?
o Is the infrastructure highly developed or is this a remote region?
o Are there climatic clues?
o If there are people in any of the slides, are there clues from ethnicity or costume?

After a while, students will build up their own bank of enquiry questions.

Follow up the initial preview by asking the students to identify where in the world you are focusing on. Insist that the students state why they have come to that conclusion. What were the helpful visual clues, what did they find misleading?

JIGSAWS

An activity using jigsaws requires movement. As a kinaesthetic activity, it will be of particular benefit to students who enjoy using visual signals, who find it reassuring to collaborate with others in order to solve problems, and who enjoy moving around. Given that the starter activity requires some preparation before students enter the room, and that it involves movement around the room, it may not be an ideal starter for a lesson that in itself requires significant use of resources. It may, on the other hand, be an ideal activity for starting a lesson that will largely be sedentary, such as feedback following an assessment, or when students will be watching an extended video while taking extensive notes (see Idea 21). Teachers will need to weigh up the educational advantages to be gained from using a starter activity that requires collaboration and movement against the potential problems associated with loosening control and allowing undirected social interaction.

For the topic you have been studying, or the new topic about to be studied, find a large photograph which represents the topic. Laminate the photograph and cut it up into eight jigsaw pieces. Put a number from 1 to 8 on the back of each fragment. Put students in pairs initially. Each pair should study the jigsaw piece carefully and try to ascertain what it is about. After a short period, ask the pair to join another pair with an adjacent number – that is, 1 joins with 2, 3 joins with 4, etc. Ask the same question. Now ask 1 and 2 to join with 3 and 4. Ask the same question for a third time. Take the task through to the final stage by getting all sixteen students together to complete the jigsaw. The task generates mystery, there is lots of collaboration and it is kinaesthetic.

If this starter activity is used at the end of a unit, students will benefit from the fact that pre-learned information has been reinforced. If the starter activity is used to launch a new topic, students will embark on the work with useful contextual information.

Cartoons are an invaluable resource for all geography teachers. They can play an important role in any part of the lesson (see Idea 28 in the section on lesson activities). At the start of any lesson, you can tap into students' enthusiasm by asking them to study them and interpret what the cartoon is attempting to show. Cartoons are easily displayed, either via a large poster or by using your laptop and projector. The brain is warmed up very effectively when questions are posed to the students as they study the cartoon.

Teachers who have the most basic skills in using PowerPoint can have the cartoon as the backdrop and timed questions flying in to challenge the students. Try to ask 'open' questions when you shape these challenges.

In discussion, students should be expected to justify the way that they interpret the cartoon. One example is provided below; it would be used with a GCSE group. The number of each question refers to the sequence in which the questions would 'fly in'.

1 What do you understand by the terms used on the cartoon? LEDC, MEDC, PRIMARY PRODUCTS.

2 Describe what happens when the oil barrel is pulled away.

3 Do you think that this is a true representation of what will happen around the globe?

4 How far do you think the cartoonist has succeeded in getting over the message? In your opinion, has the issue been exaggerated?

'Dingbats' is a visual starter activity that can be used to stretch students from Key Stage 3 through to A level. The degree of sophistication will certainly depend on the ability of the students, but students respond well when they are given two of these activities to work on; signal one as 'easy', the other as 'hard'. Most students find the exercise great fun. For the most part, the activity keeps students focused when they have to work out the geographical word or phrase hidden in the drawing or diagram provided for them. As an alternative, you can provide your students with a geographical word or phrase and the onus is on them to design a dingbat. This second approach is more likely to be successful after they have tried to solve a number of dingbats created for them.

Students will appreciate being told if the word or phrase at the heart of the dingbat stems from work they have recently covered (so that they will have a sound starting point for their deliberations). If the dingbat is used to introduce a new theme or topic, students will find it much more demanding.

Teachers will be relieved to know that you can download a wide selection of dingbats (related to geography) from the Internet. To access them, try searching using the search words 'visual geography + dingbats'. Have fun!

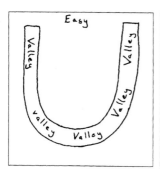

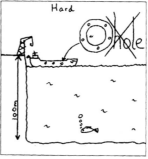

Lesson activities

GENERAL CONSIDERATIONS

In this section a wide range of ideas are suggested to encourage you to vary the kind of activities you base your learning programme around. As stated in the Section 2, 'Starters', the teacher who recognizes the value of shaping the learning programme around a combination of visual, auditory, kinaesthetic and collaborative experiences is a teacher who will access the full range of students' learning strengths. Geography as a subject allows the teacher to use and experiment with a wide variety of learning techniques. As the National Learning Strategy recognizes, the subject lends itself to the use of role-play, drama, debate, imagination, exploration, simulations, etc. Moreover, geography forms a central plank in developing literacy, numeracy and ICT skills. The fact that geographers can call on a wealth of visual materials to support each lesson and the fact that we can stimulate thinking because we teach about the wonders and extremes of our planet are further reasons why geography lessons should enthuse and stimulate students. Ideas 19 to 36 suggest a range of lesson activities used successfully in geography lessons. There will always be times when a more conservative approach to lessons is appropriate, perhaps when you are seeing students on an individual basis to provide formative feedback following an assessment. It is quite appropriate that some learning activity might be based around finding out from a standard text, using prompt questions. Variety is of course the key to a successful learning programme.

There is nothing more refreshing than watching highly skilled but newly qualified teachers perform in the classroom. As long as geographers who are much longer in the tooth can avoid feeling threatened by innovation, they can learn so much from their younger colleagues. The development of 'thinking skills' in education and the work of authors such as David Leat in recent years have done much to stimulate thinking about geography teaching. Young teachers enter the profession with interesting ideas about their teaching strategies. They recognize that we should shape our geography teaching by considering how students learn and how they enjoy learning in geography, particularly when teachers take risks with new learning strategies. Some of the starter activities and the lesson activities suggested were inspired by the call to refresh our approach to teaching and learning. Why not consider developing activities on a professional day to stimulate debate in your department? Two essential books to have in your department library will not only provide you with great geography teaching materials, but provide the foundation for professional development exercises.

○ *Thinking Through Geography* by David Leat – ISBN 1 899857 99 0
○ *More Thinking Through Geography* by Adam Nichols and David Kinninment – ISBN 1 899857 43 5

Both are published by Chris Kington Publishing.

INNOVATION AND THINKING SKILLS

No matter what key stage you are involved in, there is a tendency for students to acquire knowledge and understanding of geography without really gaining a 'sense of place'. This is particularly evident as students increasingly learn through thematic studies (tourism, crime, hydrology, transport, etc.) or through focused case studies illustrating a particular concept (e.g. urbanization, comparing São Paulo and Mexico City with London and Sydney). Consequently, this idea promotes the thought that students should be frequently challenged with gaining a sense of place ahead of learning the specifics about a focused case study or a generalized theme.

There are two key elements to this idea:

o Students can be shown the location of the place through a series of sequenced maps. Start with the location within a global setting, move through to the continent, through to the country, then region and sub-region. As the maps used to illustrate this are sequenced, take time to highlight the notion of scale and distance, dramatic topological features, significant 'human' aspects and possibly how the location has featured in the media in recent times. Combine this with:

o Contextual facts and figures about the case study/location focus. These are readily available to you from sources such as the CIA *World Factbook*. Display the contextual data in the classroom as a reminder to students while they pursue more focused lines of inquiry.

There are many occasions when geography students are expected to articulate their thoughts and ideas through extended writing. Primary colleagues have a great deal of experience in using writing frames or scaffold techniques to support and encourage extended prose. Secondary teachers, including teachers of A-level students, should recognize the value of such aids to help structure, extend and sometimes restrict prose.

Writing frames can be differentiated. At a basic level, some require 'filling in the gaps'; others provide 'key words' for inclusion in each paragraph or section. Yet others serve to ask open-ended questions at pertinent points in the text. Care should be taken in the construction of the writing frame, as you need to prevent the task turning into a comprehension exercise. Some teachers are concerned that the use of writing frames may be restrictive, particularly for those students who have well-developed organizing and communication skills. Suggest that the use of the writing frame is voluntary; those who most need it will probably use it.

The following example illustrates how a group of less able students were supported following a field trip to Spitalfields in London. They were asked to compare the area with the environment around their own school (in suburban Ipswich):

In a number of ways, Spitalfields and suburban Ipswich are very different.

For example, Spitalfields has lots of _____ , whereas Ipswich has _____

The biggest difference was _____ I think the best thing about living in Spitalfields would be _____ , but the worst thing would be _____ .

In one way, the areas were similar in that _____ .

Listening frames are invaluable when you show videos or DVDs to your class or to individuals. The aim is simple:

o to focus their listening;
o to help them pick out the main points of the video or DVD.

The example below is the simplest kind of listening frame. It was devised to help students while they watched a DVD on the impact of counter-urbanization on a satellite village outside Bury St Edmunds. This listening frame could easily be further developed:

o It could be differentiated in terms of language and complexity.
o Target groups within the class could be given different listening frames to share the burden of note-taking (this is particularly important if the video is fast-moving with extensive dialogue).
o Target groups could focus on clearly identified aspects of the topic. In this case, one frame could be devised to help record details relating to 'physical change in the village', a second could focus on different attitudes to growth, and a third could focus on the growth and decline of identified services within the village.

The Impact of Counter-Urbanization on the Village of Thurston

	Physical Changes	Service Changes	Attitudes
1970–1990			Existing elderly resident
			Local pub landlord
			Neighbouring farmer
1991–Present			Existing elderly resident
			Local pub landlord
			Neighbouring farmer

This idea enables the teacher to ascertain whether students have acquired knowledge from studying a particular case study or topic. It will also confirm whether students have also *understood* the work. The sequencing exercise can be as sophisticated as you like; it can be used through every key stage. It can be used after studying a multitude of topics or case studies. The idea is best understood through exemplification.

A GCSE class has studied ways in which city planners (perhaps in São Paulo) have attempted to alleviate the worst problems associated with rapid urbanization. Typically, city authorities with limited funds combine 'site and service schemes' with 'self-help schemes', in which a basic infrastructure is prepared by the authorities (i.e. sanitation and electricity), ready for when new residents arrive and construct basic homes themselves, under the direction of an expert. To be certain that students have understood the ideas and the logistics required to combat rapid urbanization, students are asked to sequence the following statements. Less able students could be supported with the use of a framework for sequencing (as shown).

THE STATEMENTS (THEY ARE NOT THE FRAMEWORK IN SEQUENTIAL ORDER HERE)

- Newcomers move in.
- Foundations are prepared.
- Materials (sand, cement, bricks, etc.) are supplied.
- Electricity cables are laid.
- An expert gives advice on build techniques.
- Water and sewerage pipes are laid.
- Newcomers start building basic homes.

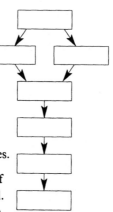

If students have a good understanding of the topic, the sequence should be logical. Knowledge of terms (e.g. sanitation) can be reinforced during the exercise.

SEQUENCING WITH CLIMATE GRAPHS

Students find it difficult to get the most out of climate graphs at the best of times. This idea considers strategies to enable them to interpret and apply information from a standard climate graph. It also suggests a simple technique to help students sequence events and relate those events to seasonal change.

When students look at climate graphs, we need to remind ourselves that they are attempting to process simultaneously a range of interrelated data (precipitation, temperature and the passage of time). At the same time, we have an expectation that they can relate these data to their own experience of a temperate climate. Moreover, we require them to consider additional factors such as seasonality, location (particularly when the climate graph is from the southern hemisphere) and the notion of a 'growing season'. In this example, students are expected to use and apply climatic data for Tsandi, Namibia. They have to sequence people's activities on the basis of a menu of alternatives provided for them. Match the lettered statements with the sequence of numbers on the climate graph.

a Farmers gather in crops and take advantage of more moderate temperatures.

b Crops begin to ripen in the warm temperatures and declining rainfall.

c Village festivals are held to celebrate the return of significant rain.

d Life is harsh as temperatures rise and water supplies fail.

e Work is difficult as the temperatures are high and the atmosphere is humid.

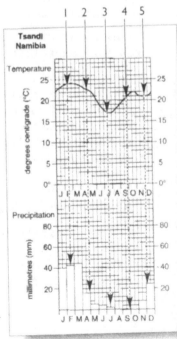

You can make the exercise as sophisticated or as challenging as you like.

USING MIND MAPS

Mind maps are a great way to enhance learning in geography. Since Tony Buzon promoted their use in the early 1990s, educationalists have continually recommended them for use in the classroom and as a tool to enhance revision programmes. Presenting information graphically (combining pictures and diagrammatic sequences with summary text) enables students to:

○ gain an overview of complex material;
○ plan more easily through thought organization;
○ solve problems;
○ develop more creative thoughts beyond the original material.

While the experts tell us that mind maps are particularly useful to 'visual learners' (including many boys), the fact that they require you to use both sides of the brain allows you to think more effectively. In a subject such as geography, they are invaluable. You will recognize the advantages of using the example overleaf, as an aid to revision or as a summary. Students get the most out of mind maps in the formative phase when, with your assistance, they are being constructed.

There are no prizes for the quality of artwork used on mind maps; as can be seen below, they are often sketched out at speed. This particular mind map is incomplete; it is for illustrative purposes only.

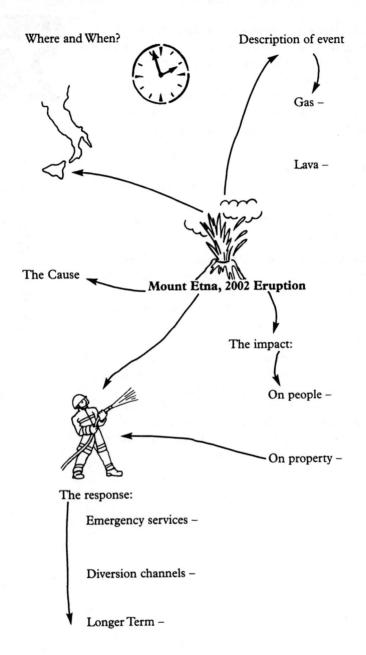

Where and When?

Description of event

Gas –

Lava –

The Cause

Mount Etna, 2002 Eruption

The impact:

On people –

On property –

The response:

Emergency services –

Diversion channels –

Longer Term –

Letter writing is an ideal mode of presentation when you want students to write in a persuasive style or if you want them to write from a biased perspective. Students who have difficulties organizing their ideas may benefit from using a writing frame (see Idea 20).

Letter writing works particularly well when a topic under study is drawing to a conclusion. A sense of place has been achieved, students have acquired some detailed knowledge of the issue; their understanding is secure after exploring a range of views. Students can write the letter with feeling, from a particular stance. To illustrate this:

Students have been studying coastal erosion along the Holderness coast of Yorkshire. They understand the cause of the erosion and they see that some areas of coast have been protected by the construction of expensive sea defences. They recognize that the construction of sea defences in one location can compound the problems of erosion elsewhere. They understand that the local authorities and the Environment Agency are reluctant to increase sea defences following a cost–benefit analysis.

○ Students could write a letter of complaint to the local council as if from an individual whose land is under threat from accelerated erosion.

○ Alternatively, they could write as a local taxpayer who lives some distance away from the threatened area, appealing against the prospect of increased council taxes.

○ Students could be asked to develop their work by writing a second, follow-up letter in response to another student's initial work.

The newspaper format is a mode of presentation that has become very popular with geography teachers. This is not surprising, as it is an ideal format when the topic being studied is controversial.

o A bypass is required. Three options have been suggested, each of which involves controversy.
o An area of coastline is eroding. Marine defences are an option, but they are very expensive.

The use of an 'editorial' is the perfect addition. After a student has reported on the issue and structured the report to ensure that a range of views are explored, his or her own view can be reported as if through the editor's comment. The students may not appreciate that you are attempting to develop higher-level skills, including that of synthesis.

Students find the 'front-page format' interesting. It allows them to experiment with hard-hitting headlines (in either the tabloid or the broadsheet format). Columns and paragraphs, combined with sub-headings, allow them to see structure in their prose. As a development, the insertion of illustrations (or cartoons) can provide them with another challenge.

Experience shows that students can become very preoccupied with design rather than content. This is particularly true if you are combining the exercise with information and communications technology (ICT) skill development. Prepare a template on an A3 sheet (if the report is to be handwritten), or in Word or Publisher if ICT is to be used. This will limit the time students spend on presentational issues; geographical content needs to be the key element.

Matching exercises are helpful activities in a number of contexts:

o At the start of a new topic, you may want to know how much knowledge students have retained from a previous key stage.

o You may want to use them at the start of a new topic. You are aware that the science department has already covered the topic, for example, ecosystems and/or the exploitation of fossil fuels and the 'greenhouse' debate. However, you are not certain about the students' level of understanding with regard to management and the impact on people.

o You want to use the matching exercise as a simple yet effective check mechanism at the end of a unit of study.

There is ample scope to differentiate the definitions to be linked to the key words or phrases. The exercise is invaluable for certain students, perhaps those who have English as an additional language.

A basic example illustrates the idea. Draw a line to match the words with their correct definition:

Key words	Definitions
Biodiversity	A representation of the complex feeding links within an ecosystem.
Food web	A way of using resources to meet the needs of the present, without preventing future generations meeting their own needs.
Ecosystem	Taking and using resources for profit.
Exploitation	The range of species of plants and animals found in an area.
Sustainable exploitation	The links that exist in an area between living things and their environment.

MATCHING WORDS AND PHRASES TO DEFINITIONS

Reference to the use of cartoons was made in Idea 15. They are an invaluable resource for geography teachers and are used in most good geography textbooks. They can be used as the main resource in the lesson. The best cartoons are clear and simple, and use exaggeration to emphasize a specific point. Students of all ages and abilities can learn from them. More often than not, they are used to reinforce knowledge and understanding already acquired. At the highest level, they can be used to further develop critical analysis. Students would be expected to interpret the message portrayed in the cartoon, but in addition they would be asked to comment on how the artist has attempted to emphasize a particular issue or to relay a specific message. Moreover, the student might be expected to comment critically on the portrayal. At a more simplistic level, cartoons can be used with much younger or with less able students as a catalyst for discussion about message and/or motive.

In the example, students are further challenged by the need to comment on similarities and differences between cartoons. Prior to viewing these cartoons, GCSE students had been studying population issues in less developed countries, particularly the causes and effects of urbanization.

TALKING HEADS

A good idea to help students absorb and sort information is to use 'talking heads'. They are particularly useful when the alternative is to provide students with dense, extended text. Some students are reluctant readers and the sight of extended text may reduce their willingness and/or capacity to select, sort and comprehend geographical information. Talking heads are particularly useful if the topic involves a controversial issue where there are a number of different views or where an individual is articulating the costs and the benefits of a decision or plan of action. Whether you select your talking head characters from a commercial source or draw the characters yourself, be sensitive to ethnicity, age and sex.

Not only will students access textual information more easily because it has been sifted and broken down for them, but their understanding is facilitated because they can relate the information to an image. One development of this idea is to ask your students to complete the text within a speech bubble:

My students find them useful because . . .

Talking heads really help me because . . .

I agree, but you need to use them with care, because sometimes . . .

It is possible to reverse the exercise. Provide students with a range of talking heads (the images need to be appropriate to the task or topic) and ask them to sift and sort an extended piece of text to show a range of different views that may stem from the information you have provided. Students allocate each selected/sorted statement to an appropriate image.

I AGREE/I DISAGREE

Many of the themes and topics studied in this subject are based around controversy and differences of opinion. Should Stansted Airport have a second runway? Is the development of the Three Gorges Dam in China having a positive impact on local people?

One lesson activity to facilitate the development of skills required in oral participation is outlined below. For illustrative purposes, assume that the class has watched a video on the destruction of the Amazonian rainforest. The programme is based around the extraction of iron ore deposits in the heart of indigenous Indian lands.

Place four large cards, one in each corner of the classroom. One card states 'I strongly agree', another states 'I agree', a third states 'I strongly disagree' and the final card states 'I disagree'. Now reveal one of four statements, using the OHP. For illustrative purposes, the statements might read:

○ The development of iron ore in this area benefits all of the people of Brazil.
○ The economic advantages of iron ore extraction outweigh the environmental consequences.
○ The extraction of minerals on indigenous Indian land should be made illegal.
○ It is easy for the Brazilian government to protect indigenous Indians from exploitation.

After each statement is revealed (one at a time), members of the class are asked to move towards the card that matches their own view. The subtlety is in the degree of 'agree'/'strongly agree' (or vice versa), and the care with which each of the four statements is created by the teacher. When the students have moved to their chosen viewpoint, having seen each of the statements, individuals are asked to justify their stance. The teacher can probe for understanding through questioning; he or she can set up a two-way argument by tempting others who are standing elsewhere to contribute.

Idea 30 has been used very successfully with senior students. However, the same idea can also be used effectively with much younger students and/or with those with learning difficulties. Students with special educational needs (SEN) are often fascinated by many of the geographical issues we study. They are enthusiastic to engage in debate and discussion. However, they can quickly get frustrated when we require them to show and develop their knowledge and understanding through written work. The exercise below shows how you can engage the students, develop their knowledge and understanding, and, at the same time, develop their oral skills.

Teachers often find that students with special needs are quick to offer a viewpoint. However, they also know that their views are often based on a gut reaction; they do not internalize or think through the issue. This exercise challenges them to do just that. In addition, it also requires them to justify their views.

Students have been given several photographs of a very run-down inner-city area. The teacher has produced a number of statements:

○ The area is better than the area we live in.
○ The area is a good place to live.
○ The best thing about the area is the shops.
○ The worst thing about the area is the lack of play space.

The statements are by necessity simplistic, but open-ended. Reveal them one at a time and ask students to move towards the card that matches their view. They enjoy the mobility and can see at a glance who agrees with them, and to what degree. They particularly enjoy the ensuing debate when opposite views are called upon.

I AGREE/I DISAGREE: MAKING IT WORK WITH SEN STUDENTS

JUSTIFYING OPINIONS

Throughout Key Stages 3–5, geography students are confronted with many controversial issues where reasoned opinion is required. After investigating and evaluating a range of alternative views or after weighing up the costs and benefits of a range of alternative solutions, students are expected to articulate their own view and justify why they hold that view. Two contrasting scenarios provide a context for you:

o Bangladesh continues to suffer from flood problems. A range of solutions are available to alleviate the problems, but not all can be initiated, owing to lack of funds. Which scheme would students select as a priority?

o The economy of British Columbia (Canada) needs a boost; unemployment has reached unacceptable levels. The government seeks to support schemes that are sustainable (both economically and environmentally). However, large reserves of oil and natural gas offer an immediate solution. What would students recommend?

These prompts will enable students to organize their thinking and shape their opinions. They provide a framework for justification.

o Highlight the main advantages of your selected scheme(s).

o State why alternative ideas or proposals have been rejected.

o Try to build in a social, economic and environmental perspective.

o Try to state the short-, medium- and long-term implications of your ideas.

o Recognize any groups or individuals who may not be happy with your decision.

o Suggest ways of appeasing those who might oppose the plan.

Ordnance Survey maps are one of the essential resources used by geography teachers across each key stage. Every successful department will have a bank of maps, at a range of scales, to enhance learning in its teachers' lessons. The learning objective in some lessons will be to develop map-reading skills. In others, the focus will be on the use and application of maps to develop knowledge and understanding on a particular theme.

Ordering class sets can be expensive, so carefully catalogue and make use of the extracts used in GCSE and GCE exams. Better still, take advantage of the fantastic annual offer of free 1:25,000 Explorer Maps for every Year 7 student in your school. You can either respond to the letter of invitation sent out by the Ordnance Survey each autumn, or contact 'customer service centre' on 08456 05 05 05. You will need to supply a few basic details, including a named liaison teacher in your department. It's that simple!

While I am promoting the outstanding services of the Ordnance Survey, take advantage of their excellent free colour guide *Map Reading Made Easy (Peasy)*. Copies can be obtained from the number above, or a pdf version may be downloaded from their website. The clear and concise guide covers every aspect you would expect, from grid references to scale to symbols.

IDEA

33

USING ORDNANCE SURVEY MAPS: A VALUABLE TOOL

To enable teachers to develop map skills in context, there are hundreds of commercial texts available. Students across each key stage and of all abilities can use and apply maps to develop knowledge and understanding across a plethora of themes and topics. Examples include:

o contrasting coastal landforms;
o identifying development sites for a new superstore;
o comparing and contrasting urban neighbourhoods;
o identifying potential reservoir sites.

An interesting development on the theme of using and applying map skills is suggested on the Ordnance Survey website. Follow the links through 'education' and 'teaching resources' to arrive at the 'dangerous road' activity. The activity will help students:

o to use six-figure grid references;
o to devise and follow routes;
o to identify map features; and
o to use a map to inform decision-making.

Students imagine that they are in a police control room. Following a road accident, they need to decide on a course of action. Information is gradually relayed to them in a series of sequenced reports. They need to make decisions about keeping traffic moving, using diversions. They may also need to consider the impact on other forms of travel. Resources to support the exercise are free to download. Teachers will quickly appreciate the multitude of other skills to be developed during the exercise.

In addition to acquiring and developing map skills, students can have great fun applying this knowledge. The Ordnance Survey website provides you with a free and easily accessed exercise to illustrate this. From their home page, go to the 'education' link then to 'teaching resources' then to 'fantasy expedition'.

This free-to-download pdf resource was commissioned by the Ordnance Survey and produced by the Geographical Association. It is an ideal resource for use with Year 7 students who have received their free 1:25,000 Explorer map (see Idea 33). The exercise allows students to develop their groupwork skills alongside their mapwork skills. Experience shows that Year 7 students find the exercise interesting and a great deal of fun.

Students can select one of two exercises to plan an expedition within their local area. They have to work within tight parameters and must fulfil a number of obligations in planning the trip. The exercise is teacher- and student-friendly, in that the resources are clear and concise. Students are supported by a carefully designed writing frame and challenged by extension tasks. Have fun!

IDEA 35

USING ORDNANCE SURVEY MAPS: LEARNING IS FUN

Students enjoy the exposure to other forms of media through their geography lessons. It has always been possible to use music and films for a specific purpose in geography lessons, but with the advent of video and sound clips in software such as Microsoft PowerPoint, it has never been easier to select image or sound extracts to enhance the study of different geographical themes. The short list below will serve to illustrate how you can match media to specific themes.

MUSIC

o Use extracts from Joni Mitchell's 'Big Yellow Taxi' when studying topics about the unsustainable exploitation of the earth's resources.

o Use extracts from UB40's 'I Am a One in Ten' when viewing the impact of unemployment on a region.

o Use extracts from some of Vaughan Williams's symphonies to create background moods when studying coastal landforms (the 'Sea' Symphony), urban growth (the 'London' Symphony) and wilderness landscapes (Sinfonia Antarctica).

TELEVISION

o Use the opening sequences from *EastEnders* and *Coronation Street* to launch the topic of urban zones.

FILMS WITH SOUNDTRACK

o Use extracts from the film *Dangerous Minds* when exploring urban decay issues in the USA. One song on the soundtrack, 'Gangsta's Paradise', written by Stevie Wonder and performed by Coolio, adds to the atmosphere (edit for mild bad language).

The classroom environment

THE WELL-EQUIPPED GEOGRAPHY ROOM

Geographers know that the subject lends itself to the use and application of a wide range of media. More than most other subjects, teaching and learning programmes are enriched by access to a rich array of materials which allow teachers to enhance their lessons through stimulating, colourful and up-to-date resources.

Geography classrooms should be set up to maximize this potential. Ideally, standard equipment should ensure that teachers and students can:

o use sophisticated equipment to facilitate the delivery of the teaching programme;
o readily access up-to-date information systems;
o make the most of presentational opportunities to reflect the learning outcomes.

To this end, an ambitious teacher will work towards equipping his or her room with:

o laptop–projector combination in association with an interactive whiteboard; ·
o access to the Internet through a broadband connection;
o video/DVD/sound system set up through a projector;
o PC and colour printing facility.

While this might appear to be an ambitious programme for some departments, schools that have already supported teachers with this investment confirm the significant gains in learning outcomes and significant increases in recruitment to GCSE and A-level courses.

The key to room layout is to be flexible. As far as the room allows, be prepared to change seating patterns, layout, and the orientation of desks on a regular basis. The determining factor should be the nature of the learning programme planned for that particular lesson or sequence of lessons.

A lesson involving whole-class debate, perhaps on trade versus aid, will be optimized when students can readily make eye contact with each other and when the teacher can move among the students to facilitate the ebb and flow of conversation. The presence of desks throughout the room may be a barrier to enthusiastic dialogue and participation. Alternatively, a regimented seating plan may prove to be ideal if the focus of the learning activity involves a period of intensive thinking, where each student has his or her own differentiated materials and prompt questions. As a teacher, you may have deliberately provided resources that have polarized messages and/or bias within them and you are anxious that in the research phase, students are not able to see all sides of an issue. Experience has shown that this works particularly well when topics such as the costs and benefits of multinationals locating in less developed countries are being studied. The impact of subsequent debate is enhanced when students are reporting very different perspectives.

It is highly recommended that students' work forms part of the classroom display. When this is the case, the learning environment is enhanced for a number of reasons:

o Students genuinely feel gratified if their work is publicly celebrated.
o Subsequent classes can see at first hand what the minimal expectations are for a particular piece of work.
o It may be an opportunity to show how the assessment criteria have been applied to a range of outcomes.
o It may be the ideal time to reinforce how whole-school policies are reflected in the marking and assessment of a particular piece of work (perhaps an aspect of the numeracy or literacy policy).

Geography lends itself to effective, eye-catching displays. Students are drawn in to displays that feature extensive graphic material rather than dense text. The complete array of presentational styles can form the basis of students' displayed work. Some examples are:

o annotated maps showing contrasting views on road bypass alternatives;
o spider diagrams showing the impact of over-exploitation of an ecosystem;
o a montage of photographs showing perspectives on life in a distant country;
o tabloid front pages reporting on the cause and effect of a flash flood;
o talking heads giving different perspectives following reports of a proposed airport expansion.

Find a prominent space in the room to display definitions of key geographical words. Change them on a regular basis. Students find it useful to have a simpler definition alongside a more complex definition. Two examples illustrate this:

EL NIÑO

1 'El Niño' is a term used to explain the cause of unusual weather events around the world. Violent rainstorms occur in some places while others face severe droughts. The cause is thought to be the occasional change in the way ocean currents circulate in parts of the Pacific.

2 'El Niño' is the Spanish name given to an occasional reversal in ocean currents in the Pacific. The warming of the eastern tropical Pacific causes large-scale changes in the atmosphere. Rainfall increases dramatically in Ecuador and northern Peru, causing coastal flooding and erosion. At the same time, droughts and forest fires are caused in Indonesia, Australia and north-eastern South America. During the stronger El Niño episodes, severe winter weather can be caused in North and South America.

HUMAN DEVELOPMENT INDEX

1 The Human Development Index is a way of measuring the quality of people's lives. Each country is given a score of between 0 and 1. The figure is worked out by combining information about how long people are expected to live, the quality of their education and the average wealth of each person in the country.

2 The Human Development Index is a weighted mix of indices that show longevity (life expectancy), knowledge (adult literacy and education) and standard of living (GDP per capita).

DISPLAYING DEFINITIONS OF KEY GEOGRAPHICAL WORDS

DISPLAY USING WALL MAPS

At the risk of appearing old-fashioned, I suggest the idea of using wall maps as a prominent feature in the classroom environment. Students enjoy using them; they can be a useful learning tool in most lessons. Careful selection of the maps intended for permanent display will give the students a sense of place. As a minimum, a world political and physical map is a must. Drawing students in, a political and physical map of Europe, set against a political and physical map of the United Kingdom, is ideal. Finally, a regional or local map completes the picture.

With careful thought to layout and with the maps annotated with thought-provoking questions and/or statements, they serve to engage and challenge the students. The questions that can be asked include:

o Which continent is this in?
o How far is it from London?
o Is the country a less economically developed country (LEDC) or a more economically developed country (MEDC)?
o Will the issue create border disputes?
o Is the area a sensitive environment?

At all times they can be used to focus minds on the range of case-study material being studied at any moment in time.

There are many companies providing these valuable resources. If your stash of publishers' catalogues has gone missing, try searching on the Internet. A simple search for 'wall maps + geography + schools' will give you more than you will ever need. You can view them before purchase, and you will notice the wealth of thematic wall maps available on topics such as population, trade and aid, ecosystems, and landforms, to name just a few.

Every geography classroom should have a bank of outline maps, readily accessible to students on a needs basis. It is a good idea to dedicate a tray cabinet to store hard copies of the following:

Blank world outline	Political world outline	Base physical world outline
Europe outline	Political Europe outline	Base physical Europe outline
UK outline	Political UK outline	Base physical UK outline
The local regional outline	Outline of the largest urban area	Outline of the school location

Electronic copies of these should also be stored for students to select and paste into their work. Most schools will have a file on their intranet (see Idea 85).

The maps can be created by teaching staff, but a better option is to search the Web for free materials for schools. A good starting point is to download the core maps for the updated 2001 National Curriculum (Key Stages 2 and 3). These are available direct from the Ordnance Survey website. Go to 'education', then 'teaching resources', then 'QCA mapping'. These maps are produced in colour A4 format. As with all of the maps in your 'bank', it is worth building the bank around A3, A4 and A5 formats.

A BANK OF OUTLINE MAPS

Field trips

Ask any former student what he or she remembers about his or her time at school, and participation on field trips will be high on the list. There is no doubt that educational visits form some of the most memorable experiences of any student at school. For the teacher, they involve an enormous amount of preparation and sometimes exasperation. Until the trip is over, even the most experienced of geography teachers will worry that things might go wrong. If the case for geography field trips can easily be made, staff involved in their planning and execution must be aware of the legal context that surrounds them. Working with students out of school brings significant additional responsibilities.

There is a great deal of guidance available for geography teachers from local authorities and from national bodies. Geography teachers must follow this advice. The aim of this section is to offer advice about key elements of the trip. It is written very much from the teacher perspective. The following questions provide a good starting point:

o Has outline permission for the trip been gained from the headteacher?
o Do you have a copy of the written school procedure for arranging trips?
o Has a risk assessment been carried out?
o Will adequate insurance cover be included in the trip?
o Will required forms be completed before the initial outreach letter is sent to parents?
o Have staff who will be required to go on the trip been approached?

While there are still many other things to consider, if the answer to each of the above questions is YES, proceed with confidence.

While geography teachers recognize the worth of field trips, from many different angles, they are acutely aware of the issues when things go wrong. Nothing will ever guarantee a stress-free trip, but good preparation in advance of the trip with regard to health and safety will cover most possibilities. Risk assessment is underpinned by the following questions:

- Does the trip present any specific hazards for students and staff (e.g. coastal fieldwork)?
- What will staff do to reduce the hazard to an acceptable level?
- How will the group leader ensure that the agreed safety measures are carried out by all members of staff on the trip?
- Where outside coach companies are used, does the school have a copy of their own safety procedures?
- What are the procedures if an emergency arises (e.g. illness on a foreign field trip)?
- How informed are students and their parents of the potential hazards, the safety precautions and the emergency procedures?

Many factors will determine the answers to these questions, not least the type of visit, the age and number of the students involved, the medical needs or special needs of individuals participating, and the location and timing of the field trip. For the most part, a risk assessment can be carried out on the basis of existing knowledge. However, there may be times when it is reasonable to ask permission to make a prior visit to assess the location.

HEALTH AND SAFETY: RISK ASSESSMENT

The nature of the field trip planned will determine the content and the amount of detail required in any letter sent out to parents. A good starting point is to think as a parent. What information would you want if the school were informing you (or asking your permission) about taking your son or daughter out of school? If the launch letter is to inform parents about an ambitious trip, such as a residential field trip abroad, parents would expect fairly detailed information. If the proposed trip is modest – say, collecting data on a local housing estate – the aim of the letter is probably to secure formal permission, and consequently details will be limited. The following checklist will cover most scenarios. Give details relating to:

o the educational reason behind the trip;
o the departure and arrival times and location;
o transport arrangements;
o accommodation (if applicable);
o food and drink;
o clothing;
o itinerary;
o staffing;
o insurance;
o cost (be careful with your wording and check that the wording is in sympathy with the whole-school policy on charging for trips);
o expectations of behaviour (a useful phrase to use is 'The normal code of conduct, as stated in the school's behaviour policy, will apply');
o responsibility for valuables;
o selection of students (see Idea 48).

The group leader of any field trip should always be a teacher at the school. He or she must accept the responsibility of this position, and other staff joining the trip should recognize this. Where large numbers of staff are required to conform to the local authority's policy on staff:student ratios, it may be a good opportunity to include support staff who work in the school. Office staff, governors, technicians and classroom teaching assistants may be delighted to be asked to go as paid or unpaid colleagues. Students will be reminded that running the trip is a team effort, and they are expected to show respect for all adults participating.

With the team, be clear from the start about roles and responsibilities. Be fair to the support staff concerning their roles when sanctions have to be used; ensure they are informed of students who may need closer supervision because of special needs, medical conditions or behavioural issues. When the field trip requires support staff to work longer hours than normal, be clear from the outset whether they are volunteering without additional payment, or whether the school will recognize the need for some additional remuneration.

In addition to the staff participating, ask yourself why the following need to be kept informed of the field trip:

○ the senior member of staff responsible for cover;
○ support staff in the school office;
○ the teacher in charge of the school newsletter;
○ heads of year/Special Educational Needs Coordinator;
○ the school website manager;
○ the caretaker;
○ school canteen staff;
○ staff who will lose students from their lessons;
○ the minibus coordinator;
○ members of the geography team who are *not* going on the trip.

TEAMWORK: STAFFING THE TRIP

GEOGRAPHY STAFF: SPOILT FOR CHOICE?

The number of teaching staff willing to participate on the field trip may be greater than the number of staff required. Suppose that an A-level residential field trip is planned. Six different geography teachers contribute to the teaching programme, but staffing ratios only allow four members of staff to accompany the 40 students. Sensitivity is the key, but there are a number of essential considerations before the team is selected:

o Will the member of staff be committed to the wider additional responsibilities that go with supervision on a residential trip (corridor duty after lights out can be an onerous duty)?

o Will the member of staff accept his or her role in the planning and preparation phase?

o Is the member of staff suited to the demands of the particular trip? It may be strenuous, for example where extensive coastal survey work is required. It may require some specialist knowledge, for example if ecosystem management is an integral part of the work. There may be a large bias within the student participants (the male : female ratio).

o Consider the impact on all the students left behind at school. Who, within the geography team, could best cope with overseeing cover or supply staff?

o If it is obvious that a member of staff will be disappointed at not being asked to participate, see him or her personally before it becomes widely known who is going. Be honest about the difficulties of selection. Be clear about the criteria you used.

The aims and objectives of a particular geography trip may predetermine the students who will be going. However, some trips may be voluntary, or the trip might be a reward for good work, or to a very popular location. There are many circumstances where field trips could be oversubscribed. The selection of students can create tension and disquiet. In these circumstances:

OVERSUBSCRIBED TRIPS: SELECTING STUDENTS

- ○ Don't over-sell the trip. Play down opportunities for 'free time'. Emphasize the work requirement.
- ○ When the initial letter goes home to parents, state that the trip is likely to be oversubscribed.
- ○ Be very open about the selection procedure, say a lottery draw. Accept an initial 'cheque deposit'. Leave enough time between the deadline for deposit cheques and the lottery draw; this will avoid a scramble to leave deposits.
- ○ After the initial names have been drawn, take out the names of reserves in strict order. You may need to use them as others drop out.
- ○ Return uncashed deposit cheques immediately to the unsuccessful students.
- ○ Ensure that messages across the department are consistent. A member of staff who breaks the ground rules regarding selection can cause untold problems for the group leader. Parents will be quick to complain.

USING COMMERCIAL COMPANIES

There are many companies specializing in geography field trips. They offer a range of alternatives – for example, residential trips, foreign field trips (some to very adventurous locations), budget trips, trips with significant home comforts, etc. Increasingly they are happy to discuss very personalized packages to meet the needs of specific geographical programmes. One of the most successful field trips in my own experience, was a study of housing regeneration schemes in the Netherlands. The tour company was very helpful in organizing guest speakers, guides were provided, and access to areas normally out of bounds was secured.

A key factor in considering the use of commercial companies is cost. Economies of scale certainly seem to enable them to undercut the price of a DIY field trip.

Before embarking on this route, consider the following questions:

o Has the geography team allowed enough time to negotiate with the company, ahead of the trip?
o Will the company carry out the risk assessment on your behalf?
o Has the company published a Safety Management Scheme?
o How long has the company been in the business?
o Have colleagues in other schools been happy with the service?
o Just what does a fully inclusive package involve?
o How many 'free' staff places are allocated?
o What 24-hour emergency assistance programme does the company have?
o What is the quality of the curriculum support materials?
o Is the company registered with bonding bodies approved by the Department of Trade?

Whatever the theme underpinning a field activity, there are occasions when it is opportune to use a local expert or guide to enhance the investigation. Even with the best planning in the world, this opportunity can prove to be problematic. It may be that the 'expert':

○ is not used to talking to students of the ability level or age of those involved;
○ has not taken on board the sharply defined educational objectives of the trip and uses the student audience to tell them all he or she has ever known about the particular area of expertise;
○ assumes too much prior knowledge from the students.

It may be that your students, who are normally a lively bunch (in every sense of the word), suddenly adopt a shy and retiring persona and fail to engage when the 'expert' asks for two-way dialogue. For all concerned, these circumstances can be uncomfortable and can detract significantly from the learning experience. Be proactive in advance of meeting the guide or expert in the field. Provide him or her with:

○ a clear and concise list of the key objectives you hope to achieve;
○ a clear statement of what the students already know and understand;
○ an unambiguous statement about the ability level of the students.

Pre-select a small number of students to ask prearranged pertinent questions, just in case there is an embarrassing pause in question and answer sessions. Always intervene if the guest or expert starts to use language levels way above the students' comprehension.

USING EXPERTS/TOUR GUIDES

The materials you provide for students while they are 'in the field' underpin the educational experience you hope to create. The following checklist will ensure that most angles are covered:

o Whatever you provide, ensure that the students have seen the items in advance and know how they relate to the activity.

o Be clear from the outset what the students will do with their field notes at the end of the activity. Experience shows that for the most part it is better to collect them in, to ensure that they are available for the writing-up phase.

o The importance of having the basics of a clipboard, pencil and protective plastic sheet cannot be overestimated. Students need to know that using the back of another student, while borrowing a pen as the rain comes down, is not conducive to quality note-taking.

o Get the balance right between observation, dialogue and note-taking.

o When questionnaires are used, consider:
   a the potential fatigue shown by clients;
   b that closed answers enable easier sharing and subsequent translation or interpretation of data;
   c that the questions being asked are directly relevant to the learning objective for the field trip.

o When field sketches are required, provide the students with an outline starting point, or ask them to complete the other side of a pre-drawn sketch.

o When assessing environmental quality and/or quality of life, provide students with polarized statements. A numerically valued grid between each polarised statement will help in the interpretation and analysis of their observations.

BALANCING WORK AND PLAY ON RESIDENTIAL TRIPS

Ahead of a residential trip, students need to be clear about expectations regarding work. While some trips are set up to be overtly work related, others may be planned to combine work with leisure opportunities. The key is to be clear from the outset. Will the students need to work in the evening? Will work need to be completed on the trip itself or shortly after arriving back? Will 'free time' be based around organized activities?

Occupying students in the evenings can be the cause of stress for staff. It is worth investing the time preparing activities in advance. Experience shows that a well-planned evening has huge benefits. Students and staff have great fun, and the dividends follow through to the next day, when students are focused and ready for the next work phase.

When organizing fun activities, be prepared to lose a little dignity; students warm to staff who join in karaoke sessions. Alternatively, students love devising captions to digital pictures taken earlier in the day. A strong editorial hand might be required before the photos are projected! An old-fashioned quiz always goes down well.

On your return, it is worthwhile displaying pictures to celebrate the field trip. Ensure that you combine these with information relating to the work undertaken. You wouldn't want senior managers to get the wrong impression!

Links with other subjects

Geography and English are mutually supportive. Geographers need to know what English teachers are striving to do with their students, and vice versa. The most successful and tangible example of cooperation I have seen in recent years was when the English department asked the students to focus their GCSE-assessed oral coursework around an environmental issue. While the English department helped students to frame their talk around the key elements of 'speaking and listening skills' (see below), the geographers provided the context and the suggested route of inquiry for research.

Speaking and listening skills in both English and geography involve:

o asking and answering questions about an issue;
o describing and explaining a process;
o planning and organizing a discussion;
o presenting a point of view and engaging in debate;
o using role play and drama to understand different values and attitudes.

With regard to writing skills in English and Geography, the following aspects are involved:

o learning subject-specific terminology;
o changing writing styles to: (1) explain; (2) inform; (3) persuade; (4) express feelings;
o writing clearly and accurately for selected audiences.

Reading skills in English and geography involve:

o scanning text to find relevant information;
o extracting, inferring and deducing meaning.

You will find that English colleagues have some excellent materials to illustrate how to develop these skills. Perhaps the best examples are the materials they can provide to help students develop different writing styles. Ask them!

As with English, maths and geography are mutually supportive. Geographers need to know what maths teachers are striving to do with their students, and vice versa. In both maths and geography we ask our students to develop skills in describing and understanding spatial patterns. Particularly when we use maps, we have an expectation that the students have a basic understanding of orientation, angle and direction.

Geographers handle and manipulate data across a multitude of topics. We expect students to be able to ascertain the most effective means of displaying data in tabular or graphical form. We develop these skills through unique geographical contexts, but we should ensure that the students are getting the same advice about the use and application of mathematical data. A very simple anecdote will illustrate the need for dialogue between the two departments. It was only last year that a geography colleague was bemoaning the lack of mathematical skills of the students when he asked them to represent data for the United Kingdom and for India, to show the proportion of workers engaged in primary, secondary and tertiary industry. He could not get over the fact that the protractors he had supplied left the students confused and deskilled. Perhaps he should have been aware that the maths department had moved on to angle measures many years earlier!

Dialogue and a shared commitment to methodology will enable students to see the relevance of their learning across the curriculum.

LINKS WITH MATHS

More than for any other subject, you need to be aware of, and act upon, the links with science. Within the Key Stage 3 Programmes of Study there is clear content overlap. Students studying either science or geography are expected to learn about 'rock formation' and 'volcanic activity'. Across most of the GCSE specifications (and some A-level specifications), the theme of 'sustainability' is prominent in both geography and science. Moreover, an understanding of ecosystems and the problems associated with over-exploitation permeate both subjects.

Joint planning between the two departments is essential if you are to avoid comments from students such as 'this is boring, we've just done this in science' or 'we watched this video last year in our biology lesson'. Comments like this can undermine your confidence, particularly when students question the validity of unplanned repeats. However, curriculum overlap can be advantageous, as long as mutual planning takes place. Reinforcement of knowledge and understanding, and mutually supportive resources and expertise, can help both staff and students.

To help with your planning on this issue, a simple but effective way forward is the following:

o Agree that the science team will shape their teaching programmes around the theoretical and scientific background material. They can lay the foundations of rock formation and vulcanicity and/or ecosystem components and function.
o The geography team will develop this starting point to consider case-study material looking at the impact on people and future management issues.

Geography departments can contribute to the statutory subject of citizenship in many different ways. This idea gives a brief summary of the components of the citizenship scheme of work and the strands running through it. Geographers will recognize immediately how the subject lends itself to the delivery of citizenship.

o *Social and moral responsibility*: Pupils learn self-confidence and socially and morally responsible behaviour, both in and beyond the classroom, towards those in authority and towards each other.
o *Community involvement*: Pupils learn about becoming helpfully involved in the life and concerns of their neighbourhood and communities.
o *Political literacy*: Pupils learn about the institutions, problems and practices of our democracy and how to make themselves effective in the life of the nation, locally, regionally and nationally, through skills and values as well as knowledge.

Planning of provision should reflect the need to ensure that pupils have a clear understanding of their roles, rights and responsibilities in relation to their local, national and international communities. The three strands in the programmes of study to be taught are:

o knowledge and understanding about becoming an informed citizen;
o developing skills of inquiry and communication; and
o developing skills of participation and responsible action.

The next idea illustrates a number of geographical contexts for the delivery of the citizenship programme.

CITIZENSHIP: BE AWARE OF STATUTORY REQUIREMENTS

CITIZENSHIP: A GEOGRAPHICAL CONTEXT

Coverage of many of the components and strands in the citizenship programme of study can be achieved through a number of geographical contexts. For example, you could select a 'live' local planning issue. There may be controversy about:

o the need for a new bypass, with several alternative routes up for discussion;
o the intention to develop renewable energy supplies, with nobody wanting a proposed wind farm in their back yard;
o the local authority wanting to build a 'halfway house', to help reformed drug users in their rehabilitation; three sites are being considered, all of which have received receive a hostile reception from local residents;
o a local resident wanting to take coastal protection measures into his own hands; the local authority has decided on a policy of 'managed retreat'.

All these issues have formed the basis for decision-making exercises in my school. There are thousands of comparable examples across the country. Such issues receive significant coverage in the local media (see Idea 60). Local councillors and residents are active and available for dialogue. Access to current and pertinent planning documents is normally assured.

Develop a problem-solving exercise around one such issue. All of the components of citizenship can be included, and the strands fall into place with ease. The Department for Education and Skills (DfES) website has a dedicated citizenship link where a range of case studies are illustrated and resourced. The websites of geographical organizations such as the Geographical Association suggest a wealth of alternative ideas.

As you will be aware, geography and information and communications technology (ICT) have their own attainment targets and level descriptions in the National Curriculum. Each has a detailed (non-statutory) programme of study to provide teachers with a comprehensive guide to progression and a clear route of inquiry. However, advice from the Qualifications and Curriculum Authority suggests that schools should take these schemes of work as a starting point and look for opportunities to devise their own strategies, particularly with a view to combining units from different subjects. Their advice is clear:

Helping children make connections between subjects and transfer their learning from one subject to another is an essential part of successful curriculum planning. Connections make learning more coherent for children and help them to see the relevance of what they do.

Level descriptors alone illustrate the potential:

Pupils select the information they need for different purposes, check its accuracy and organise it in a form suitable for processing. They use ICT to structure, refine and present information in different forms and styles for specific purposes and audiences.

These strands are taken from the Level 5 descriptor in ICT. Compare this with the following, taken from the Level 5 descriptor in geography:

They select and use appropriate skills and ways of presenting information and present their findings both graphically and in writing.

The illustrative ideas provided in each of the units for each subject give a multitude of opportunities for collaboration. One example confirms this. While you are teaching unit 18 of the National Curriculum (geography), i.e. 'How the fashion industry connects people around the globe', devise a questionnaire to ascertain the source of clothing in a household. Use a spreadsheet to 'design, structure, capture and present the data' – Unit 5, ICT.

Useful contacts

IDEA

59

PARENTS ARE A USEFUL RESOURCE

Reaching out to parents through the school newsletter and school website can be surprisingly fruitful. The following examples provide evidence that parents can make a very valuable contribution to geography lessons. The geography department gave advance notice of themes and topics to be studied in future weeks. Parents were asked to offer their experiences or their expertise to enhance learning. Some of the more successful contributions are listed below:

o Study of fragile ecosystems. A parent provided an illustrated talk on setting up an eco-friendly tourist development in Belize.
o Study of declining coal-mining areas. A parent talked about the need for his family to move away from south Wales because of the impact of large-scale mining closures in the Rhondda Valley.
o Alternative routes for a relief road from Ipswich Docks. A parent (who was also a local planner) arranged for the exhibition to be housed at the school for three weeks.

As in Idea 50, whenever you arrange for a guest speaker to talk to your students, spend some time in advance preparing the ground. You will need to convey your learning objectives, the age and ability of the students and their prior knowledge. Ground rules need to be established over the numbers in the audience, hardware requirements and timing to allow questions and answers.

LOCAL RADIO

If you are prepared to plan well ahead (the media seem to want a significant planning period for their schedules) and you are happy to share your work with thousands of listeners, don't underestimate the role that local radio companies may have. You would normally seek their support and/or collaboration if you have something in particular to celebrate. Your senior managers will love the kudos that comes with radio exposure.

Use local radio as an innovative aid to your teaching programme. The students' learning will be enhanced if they are more engaged and/or enthusiastic in their work, especially when they see the opportunity of being a local celebrity for a while.

One particular thing that works well is the recording of a debate in class on a contentious local issue. The technical issues are minimal, and several students can be directly involved.

○ Perhaps there are plans for a new bypass and three options exist.
○ The council may be considering a planning application for a new site for 'travellers'.
○ An area near the school could be prone to increased flood events; the cause, impact and solutions could be debated.

EXAM BOARDS 1:
WHY BECOME AN EXAMINER/MODERATOR?

Involvement in examining has huge benefits for your teaching and consequently for the learning programmes experienced by your students:

○ You have access to detailed information to see exactly what is required of your students.

○ You will further understand the importance of command words as used in questions. When you share this information with your students, they will see how command words should prompt a given response. '*Describe* the distribution of the world's fastest-growing cities' requires a very different response compared to '*Explain* the distribution of the world's fastest-growing cities'!

○ You can acquire a bank of answers that reflect responses from students at different grade boundaries. You can use these with your students as part of your assessment for learning strategy.

○ You can build up a bank of assessment materials and mark schemes. New colleagues can receive training in the use and application of the mark scheme.

○ When moderating coursework, you will see imaginative approaches used in other schools.

○ The mode of assessment used in other centres may prompt you to change your own, to the benefit of your students. An illustrated talk on the cause and effect of rainforest exploitation may be more attractive to selected students than an extended essay.

○ You may discover new resource material.

○ You can use some of the training materials directly with your students. Your students will enjoy direct involvement in assessment for learning.

Meeting with colleagues from across the country can have significant benefits. Networking can lead to the sharing of resources and the sharing of resource development. This book has already discussed the challenges of keeping up to date with our fast-changing world and with the bewildering choice of published and online materials available to geographers. At a recent examiners' meeting I established a link that enabled me to significantly update the resources used at my centre (on the shrinking of the Aral Sea). Moreover, the colleague provided me with an assessment package that perfectly matched the assessment criteria for one of our compulsory assignments. We had been searching for an international issue that had a 'physical' and a 'human' dimension. We needed an issue where the students were required to explore a range of alternative views. A minimum of ten hours' work was saved through this contact.

Networking increases opportunities for developing links with publishers. An existing author may be looking for new colleagues to join him or her on a new writing venture or a new curriculum development project.

As we live in the age of 'threshold' and 'upper pay spine' advancement, working for exam boards and running subsequent training and/or information sessions within your centre can look really good as part of your portfolio of evidence. Geographers have plenty of opportunity to show sustained and significant contribution to the school!

EXAM BOARDS 3: MAKING CONTACT AND CURRICULUM DEVELOPMENT

The mechanism for applying to become an examiner or moderator has improved significantly in recent years. In England and Wales you can apply online through the newly formed National Assessment Agency (www.naa.org.uk). Through the NAA's dedicated geography team, the intention is to:

o offer professional development to those involved in external and internal assessment;
o provide professional recognition of the skilled work of assessment;
o disseminate good practice in geography assessment.

As an alternative, you can seek information direct from the existing examination boards: AQA (www.aqa. org.uk), Edexcel (www.edexcel.org.uk), OCR (www.ocr. org.uk) or WJEC (www.wjec.co.uk). This may be a better bet if you want to explore curriculum development work in geography, alongside examining. Recent examples of this include the development of 'entry-level' exams and the ongoing development of the new geography pilot GCSE. This is a fast-developing specification that aims to combine innovative external and internal assessment techniques, while recognizing citizenship and vocational slants. It incorporates newly developed tools, such as GIS systems (see Idea 87), within the teaching and assessment programme.

In Scotland, teachers should explore opportunities through the Scottish Qualifications Authority (www.sqa.org.uk). In Northern Ireland, seek information from the Council for Curriculum, Examinations and Assessment, Northern Ireland (www.ccea.org.uk).

There are many positives to come out of contact with charities such as CAFOD and Christian Aid. As you will see in Ideas 65 and 66, they offer a range of interesting, stimulating and up-to-date resources to enliven your teaching and learning programmes. Issues of global concern form the basis of their work, with particular emphasis on disparity, poverty, trade, disaster management and sustainable futures. Students visiting their websites will be challenged when they view the 'current campaigns' section of each site. The challenge includes learning about and understanding issues of global concern. Students will recognize what they might do, or how they might coordinate larger groups to help in campaigns.

There are opportunities for geography teachers to attend in-service training sessions to extend their own knowledge and understanding of global issues. In addition, these charities' websites provide you with many examples of well-designed and detailed assembly opportunities (see Ideas 5 and 6).

Remember these are charitable organisations. They provide you with opportunities to make donations, particularly when you download their 'free' resources. In purchasing their priced materials, you will be contributing to their fund-raising initiatives. Ideas 65 and 66 present you with a selection of their valuable educational resources. It is worth geographers regularly checking their websites (www.christian-aid.org.uk and www.cafod.org.uk) or signing up for their newsletters to keep up to date. Many of the illustrative materials selected for your consideration are particularly engaging for students, in that they involve games and simulations.

CHARITIES 1: A VALUABLE RESOURCE, A CHANCE TO MAKE A DIFFERENCE

The following excellent resources will enhance teaching and learning programmes in geography.

THE TRADING TRAINERS GAME

The focus of the Trading Trainers game is on Latin America. This lively simulation explores the way unfair trade and unstable economies directly affect the lives of ordinary people. In family groups, the players make trainers to survive. They are hounded by a loan shark and struggle to pay their bills. Downloading the game is free (but make a donation). It is aimed at students aged 13-plus.

THE CHOCOLATE TRADE GAME

The focus of the Chocolate Trade game is Ghana and the United Kingdom. The game introduces students to the difficulties experienced by workers in the chocolate trade and the benefits of fair trade policies. It is aimed at students aged 9-plus. The game can be purchased for £3.50.

TRADE RULES!

The focus of Trade Rules! is the global economy and the rules that govern international trade, the World Trade Organization and the impact of global trading systems on poorer countries. Aimed at students aged 16-plus, currently it can be purchased for £4.99.

THE DEBT GAME

Again, the focus of the Debt game is global, with international debt and the difficulties of getting out of that debt the central theme. Aimed at students aged 14-plus, currently it can be purchased for £2.50.

H2KNOW

H2knOw looks at issues concerning water around the world. The resources illustrate graphically the challenges facing the world. In understanding the issues, your students will be motivated to do something about the 1.1 billion people who do not have access to clean water. There is no charge.

CAFOD, the Catholic Agency for Overseas Development, is a charity that offers geography teachers and students a wealth of resources, all free. A few minutes spent navigating through CAFOD's website will reveal a wealth of imaginative ideas and well-presented materials, some aimed at teachers, some for students. It is very obvious that their staff who devised the materials have a very good understanding of pedagogy: they understand what stimulates students and they present their materials with clearly identified learning outcomes. If you visit the website, you will see that the list below is just a fraction of what is available.

They offer resource packs:

o Aimed at A-level geography students, a resource pack provides students with information relating to measuring development and inequality, the case study being Sierra Leone.
o Their Global Citizen pack provides a clear route of inquiry to explore issues such as fair trade and tourism concern.

They offer a teacher file:

o Their 'Get Global' guide is a skills-based research/action/evaluation pack that promotes the idea that students can take responsibility for their own independent learning.

Their factsheets cover a number of different topics. All are concise and well presented:

o Through named examples, students can see the cause and effect of various global disasters and can see how organizations such as CAFOD can offer both short-term and long-term help.
o The costs and benefits brought by multinationals to less economically developed countries.
o Why conflict over water supplies exists. The repercussions of using dirty water. Short-term and long-term solutions.

THE METEOROLOGICAL OFFICE

Keep yourself informed about the information and materials supplied by this organization. Covering an area of the geography curriculum that is conceptually difficult, the Meteorological Office's website provides you and your students with up-to-date information on climatology and meteorology. Moreover, the organization has a long-term commitment to helping geography teachers acquire new knowledge and greater understanding on this fast-developing and dynamic area of the curriculum.

The website (www.metoffice.gov.uk) is particularly easy to navigate. Links within the site provide information about current research and topical issues (e.g. global warming and climate change). There is a particularly impressive section looking at the impact of extreme weather on individuals and communities around the world.

In addition to the outstanding materials available on the website, the organization provides materials (some at no cost, others at a modest cost) for students and teachers across all key stages. At the time of writing, the following were available to support this statement:

o resources and learning activities for use in primary schools (glossary of terms, puzzles, and facts about weather and climate);
o satellite poster sets and associated meteorological maps for use at Key Stage 4;
o a free interactive, multimedia CD-ROM on global warming for use with A-level students; this highly visual resource asks rhetorical questions and answers them by using video clips, charts, animations and images.

The sustainable geography department

EDUCATION FOR SUSTAINABLE DEVELOPMENT (ESD)

In 2002 the Qualifications and Curriculum Authority published guidance for schools to help shape and nurture education for sustainable development (ESD), a vital aspect of education. Geography departments were always bound to be at the heart of this curriculum development. As geographers we are clearly well placed to take the lead in presenting opportunities for students to learn and develop their understanding of ESD. Moreover, geographers can signal and promote the opportunities inside and outside school for students to become involved as active participants in a sustainable lifestyle. The message can be modelled in the learning environment created by the geography team in terms of its practical approach to energy use, transport, waste minimization and waste recycling, among others.

Getting over the message and witnessing action are best achieved if geographers are supported by a strategic whole-school approach. The LEA should be able to offer advice and tangible support. Effective links can be fostered with individuals and groups in the local community who have like-minded intentions. Ideas 69 and 70 illustrate some simple yet effective ways in which geography departments can lead by example; the curriculum message is translated into action.

Valuable time can be spent exploring opportunities to further develop ESD in schemes of work. Careful selection of pertinent case studies will help in doing so, but there is a greater chance of students understanding and being motivated by ESD if:

o Local case studies provide them with first-hand examples of sustainable projects.
o Local ESD associations are invited into lessons to enrich the learning experience.
o After acquiring knowledge and understanding of a sustainable issue, students are required to take action. This may be simply in the form of letter-writing or lobbying. Alternatively, it could be an opportunity for them to persuade their parents to adopt a more sustainable approach at home. It could be active participation in a local community project such as recycling or reclamation, or developing an education programme with local primary schools.
o Opportunities are taken to allow students to offer their reasoned opinions about controversial issues. There are many aspects of ESD that involve heated debate and necessary sacrifice.

The international perspective should not be forgotten. ESD can be the ideal context for students to link with schools abroad. International links are the ideal way of further developing knowledge and understanding of:

o different perspectives about global issues such as global warming (cause, effect and solutions);
o interdependence, particularly the way in which trade, aid and consumption interrelate;
o sustainable issues in more fragile parts of the world where ESD is not just about choices and options but about survival.

ESD: WRITING IT INTO SCHEMES OF WORK

In addition to the curriculum avenues that are opportune to promote ESD, the geography department can be seen to take the lead in very tangible ways:

o Staff and subsequently students should be seen to be active in minimizing energy consumption. Good habits can be achieved in turning off unnecessary lights, electrical equipment, heaters, etc. Doors and windows can be closed to reduce heat loss. Good habits take time to achieve. Staff need to take the lead, but good habits spread around the school.

o A constant but necessary battle needs to be waged in favour of waste minimization, particularly when it comes to paper. Just what does happen to half-filled exercise books at the end of an academic year? What happens to the thousands of worksheets that are discarded following yet another innovation, or change to the scheme of work?

o How far do you encourage your students to lobby through their year councils for a robust whole-school recycling scheme? Not just paper needs to be recycled, but the thousands of metal drink cans and plastic bottles discarded every year in a typical high school.

o Is the purchasing policy of the department overt? Where resources are purchased using recycled material or managed sources, are the students aware of it?

o Does the thorny issue of transport to and from school receive serious debate? How effective is any campaign to change the transport habits of 'the school run'?

Homework
and revision

Setting homework in geography need not be an onerous task. Not only are there many opportunities to meet the guidelines for homework, as published by the DfES, but there are many commercial and non-commercial organizations that provide quality materials for homework tasks in the subject.

The DfES suggests that homework should be:

o A motivating factor in encouraging students to study on their own, while prioritizing and planning through extended assignments. This is particularly so in geography, where at Key Stage 4, coursework assignments permeate all specifications, and in post-16 study, where students are expected to plan, research, structure and reach conclusions on their chosen individual study.

o A chance to consolidate and reinforce skills and understanding. There are a multitude of homework exercises where students can, for example, apply map-reading skills to new locations. They can show their understanding by writing a balanced article on an emotive issue (extending nuclear power provision, perhaps).

o A chance to extend school learning through additional reading. Having studied a topic such as global warming, students could be provided with new material produced from the perspective of the emerging nations.

o A chance to involve parents, with the additional benefit of keeping them up to date with what is being studied in geography. There is no better way to do this than by collecting primary data through a parent questionnaire. A study of out-of-town shopping centres could test opinions on the costs and benefits of such schemes.

There are a wealth of materials available. For the most part they are excellent, in that they have clearly been written by teachers who are familiar with statutory programmes of study or who have an intimate knowledge of GCSE and A-level specifications.

Most leading geography publishers produce CD-ROMs dedicated to homework tasks and linked directly to the National Curriculum geography orders. Easy to navigate, the CD-ROMs provide:

o a range of differentiated activities, which can be used to stretch your more able students and support those who are struggling;
o topical case studies and a wide selection of engaging activities to really motivate pupils;
o extra resource material and up-to-date case studies to meet National Curriculum requirements on studying place;
o integrated key geographical skills exercises;
o worksheets in Word and pdf formats so you can tailor them as you require;
o teacher's notes and a National Curriculum matching chart.

The BBC includes homework tasks as an integral part of its 'Bitesize' geography materials. A wide range of themes such as population, managing ecosystems and energy are covered (twelve in all), and one exercise is dedicated to geographical skills. The tasks can be emailed and come with a clear mark scheme.

Students can either mark their own or work through the assessment with a study friend.

These materials and many more are easily accessible. Just look at the 'Ordnance Survey' website (www.ordnancesurvey.co.uk) to confirm that it's worth the time searching!

HOMEWORK: LETTING YOUR VALUABLE RESOURCES GO HOME

While encouraging your students to make optimum use of homework and at the same time providing them with first-class resources to enable them to complete the task, there is always the difficulty that valued materials can get lost. Given the tight budgets that many geographers have to work within, there is an important need to set up clear rules and check mechanisms for resources.

While it will not be long before all tasks are published on the intranet and the required resources accessed by students from home, we are not there yet. Whatever policy you have for the distribution of resources in your department, ensure that it is adhered to by all. A chain is only as strong as its weakest link. When expensive resources such as maps, colour photographs, digital cameras, etc. are loaned out, as a minimum the resources need to be numbered and allocated to specific students. This takes time, and should not be the last thought as the end-of-lesson bell sounds. Good habits regarding resource allocation can be acquired by students when systems are clear and used consistently. The same is true when collecting resources in. Students need to know exactly when they are required (especially if it is before the next lesson) and they need to know the check return mechanism.

There are many commercial materials available for students to use to help them prepare for exams across all key stages. Most of the large publishing companies produce dedicated revision guides for geography, and there are an increasing number of interactive websites dedicated to the cause. There seems to be a wide range of opinions about the value of such guides and websites. Perhaps the three main criticisms are based on the facts that:

○ some of the guides are not specification specific and students can get lost if left to their own devices;
○ they can dominate the revision period, and the teacher assumes less and less responsibility for helping students through this vital period;
○ they largely focus on knowledge and only to a lesser extent on understanding; and exam technique often comes a poor third.

Perhaps the best advice is to review several and decide how best they might complement the school-devised revision programme. The two best Internet-based packages are produced by 'Internet Geography' (follow the link to 'revision guide'), and 'BBC Bitesize Revision' (follow the link to 'geography'). Both provide students with a broad view of good revision practice (e.g. developing revision cards and using mind maps); both use multiple-choice questions to assess knowledge against prescribed mark schemes. They are not specification specific, so students will need to be trained as to what units to select. The BBC site has the added advantage of giving students feedback as to why answers they give are correct or wrong.

REVISION 2: EXAM TECHNIQUE

When you develop the revision programme in your centre, don't underestimate the need to plan dedicated lessons for exam technique. Hopefully, as part of your assessment for learning strategy, you will have prepared students over a number of years and through each topic to learn through assessment, but there is every reason to focus their thinking at the end of the course to some key principles. Do the students know:

o how many papers they will sit?
o the content/theme of each paper?
o the length of each paper?
o the mark weighting of the paper?
o the importance of understanding the command words used in each question?
o the usefulness of including sketch maps and/or diagrams?
o the importance of backing up observations with case-study knowledge?
o how levels of response mark schemes work (if appropriate)?
o the need to utilize the range of geographical skills (e.g. map/photo/graph interpretation)?
o the time to use extended prose as against bullet-point answers?
o the importance of rubric in the presentation of answers?
o the way the quality of written communication is judged?

Information and communications technology (ICT)

The development of information and communications technology (ICT) as a learning tool has been remarkable in recent years. More than any other subject, geography can use ICT to enhance learning programmes developed in school. Its use can be a great motivating factor for students, who will certainly embrace the use and application of this tool. Some staff, particularly those in the later stages of their career, may be reluctant to utilize it, perhaps because they feel that they have inadequate skills or because they are concerned that the technology will let them down at a crucial stage of the teaching programme. Experience shows that careful, planned use of ICT, with prerequisite training, can open up new horizons for staff. Reluctant staff quickly see the value of it and are rewarded with positive outcomes from their students.

It would be possible to write a whole book on the use and application of ICT in geography. The aim of this section is simply to whet your appetite and to offer several pointers about using ICT effectively and without tears. The list of ICT applications provided in Idea 77 is not exhaustive, but it serves to illustrate the wide range of opportunities available to geography teachers. Idea 78 offers a word of caution about the use of ICT in lessons. Beyond this, Ideas 80 to 83 provide more detail on selected applications.

With advanced planning, ICT can enhance learning programmes in many ways:

○ The Internet opens up a world of up-to-date material for all. By its very nature, geography is dynamic. Staff and students who are hungry for up-to-date case studies can find them with relative ease (as long as they know how to do effective searches). New materials to update existing case studies can be discovered. At a more sophisticated level, materials written from a different perspective can be explored. A-level students can access materials written outside the Eurocentric perspective.

○ Schools with well-developed intranet systems can provide a highly selective bank of materials for students to access. Research skills and outcomes are enhanced, and time is saved. Teaching staff are secure in the knowledge that materials are entirely relevant and appropriate.

○ Key tools of the geographer, such as maps, GIS systems and up-to-date databases, e.g. census materials, have never been more readily available.

○ When ICT is used with interactive whiteboards, a whole range of simulations and graphics are opened up.

○ As a tool for presentation, ICT is a real bonus. Sorting, editing, structuring, illustrating, recording, manipulating and representing data, etc. can all be done more effectively. If the students have acquired sufficient IT skills, the end product looks magnificent and is completed with optimum use of time. The geography remains the central feature.

○ Videos and, more recently, DVDs have long been a valuable learning resource. With advanced preparation, their use can be optimized.

I have already put forward many reasons why geography teachers should embrace the use of ICT in their classrooms, but it is important to introduce a note of caution. In planning the teaching programme, staff should reflect on the following:

○ Incorporating ICT into the lesson should ensure that students develop their *geographical* knowledge, understanding and skills. Developing ICT skills should not be the main learning objective.

○ Access to sufficient and reliable hardware is a key element. It will determine the success or failure of the learning objectives. Experience shows that, when using IT, sharing a work station has advantages, but it also has significant disadvantages. Are all students 'on task'? Do certain individuals dominate? Where is shared work saved? Can students readily print draft copies? If colour copies are required, who pays?

○ While IT equipment is increasingly located within subject areas, some schools have inadequate resources to match need. Some schools have dedicated IT suites located some distance away from geography rooms. If IT is being used by selected members of a teaching group and the work stations are outside the normal teaching area, who will supervise them and intervene to move learning forward? Has optimum use been made of classroom teaching assistants?

○ Have software packages and Internet sites been tried out in advance of the lesson?

○ Does a back-up plan exist if the IT equipment or the DVD player fails?

○ Are the geography team aware of the IT skill level of the students?

○ Has liaison taken place between those who shape the geography scheme of work and the ICT scheme of work?

The rapid development of the Internet has enabled geography teachers to quickly find ideas to develop their teaching programmes and resources to enhance learning activities. This section gives readers an insight as to what is available and where. A short time spent surfing the websites suggested below will confirm that there is a fantastic array of information. Much of the information and many of the resources are free. This information, combined with the fact that most of the materials and ideas stem from practising geography teachers and cutting-edge geography departments, means that your surfing will not be in vain.

The first tip in this section is to allocate time on a 'professional day' to exploring key sites. Even the most reluctant IT user in your department will quickly see the benefits of exploration.

While it is always risky to list actual websites to view (given the here today, gone tomorrow nature of some sites), those listed below are stable and the organizations behind them are in it for the long haul. They will provide you with a multitude of links to explore further. Someone needs to write an entire book about the potential for each site. Subsequent ideas in this section illustrate just how useful they are. Spend time looking at:

○ www.ncaction.org.uk/subjects/geog
○ www.curriculumonline.gov.uk/Subjects/Gg/Subject.htm
○ www.qca.org.uk/7895.html
○ www.standards.dfes.gov.uk/schemes2/secondary_geography
○ www.ictadvice.org.uk (Becta)
○ www.ngfl.gov.uk
○ www.rgs.org
○ www.geography.org.uk

THE INTERNET: GATEWAY TO A WEALTH OF RESOURCES

At www.ncaction.org.uk/subjects/geog you will find invaluable information relating to National Curriculum targets and levels, specifically with reference to:

o making judgements about students' work at the end of each key stage;
o a student portfolio of work;
o explaining how the portfolio can be used to reach a decision about levels.

Inexperienced teachers or non-specialists who have been asked to teach geography at Key Stage 3 will be able to accurately assess work produced by their students with much more confidence.

The website also provides information about ICT:

o What is ICT in geography and what are the statutory requirements?
o What ICT opportunities exist in geography?
o What are the basic recommendations about hardware and software for schools?

Use the information of this part of the website to lobby for greater access to IT facilities in your school.

As regards innovation in geography teaching, a link takes you to the QCA/GA/RSG innovation site:

o the work of 'leading geography departments';
o professional development activities using real geography examples;
o guidance from professional geographers on topics such as 'the changing British city', 'census and neighbourhood data', 'ecotourism';
o bright ideas for fieldwork;
o what to do with gifted and talented students.

Picking up tips from colleagues who are at the forefront of development work in geography is always to be recommended.

Further topics covered by the website include:

o careers and pathways through geography;
o promoting the subject in your school;
o planning, teaching and assessing the geography curriculum for students with learning difficulties.

After you recognize that the key to using the site (www.ngfl.gov.uk) is the careful use of search words ('geography' as a search word alone gives you over 500 resource hits) and after you come to appreciate the importance of the 'age guidance' logo, this site gives you access to a huge range of material for use in geography lessons. Links to the following resources are available free of charge:

o Images and background data to enhance decision-making exercises. One example for students to explore is the potential for power generation in a peat bog area of the Republic of Ireland.
o Links to a 'geography in the news' website. Direct links to a news coverage format covering world events such as World Environment Day and the impact of the South Asian tsunami.
o A case study of the River Ribble. Images and information from source to mouth explain features of the physical and human landscape.
o The 'World InfoZone'. As the site states, 'WIZ around the world'. Facts and figures and up-to-date information are provided on the geography of virtually every country.

To do the site justice, you need a full day! Why not take advantage of the free resources available to you? Think of the time it will save in terms of preparation.

THE NATIONAL GRID FOR LEARNING

After visiting the site of the Royal Geographical Society (www.rgs.org), again you will save hours of preparation time. The professional development advice is also first class. Essential information to those new to the profession is concise and accurate. While the entire site is perfect for anyone with a love of geography, the education section, written by geographers for geographers, is outstanding, and deserves the accolade and awards it has received. You could spend many hours searching the array of resources and following the extensive links to other sites. The site is continually updated, and you will find information on, for example:

o courses and continuing professional development (CPD) events for geographers to extend their own knowledge and understanding (e.g. on safety management on field trips);
o role-play exercises such as 'sweat shirt', based on the garment industry in Bandung, Indonesia;
o advice about embedding geographical information systems (GIS) in schools;
o how to enhance the teaching programmes for 'education for sustainable development';
o a Microsoft PowerPoint presentation for A-level students on 'globalisation';
o details relating to the RGS teaching grants (£800) for teachers who show imagination, innovation and creativity in their teaching.

The Geographical Association's easy-to-navigate site (www.geography.org.uk) provides you with a wealth of additional information not available on other sites:

○ Access to the content of the Association's three excellent journals written for teachers is provided:
    a *Teaching Geography* is written for secondary school teachers and contains resources, professional development opportunities, and up-to-date articles on breaking geography news.
    b *Primary Geography* is written for colleagues working in Key Stages 1 and 2. It gives very practical advice on materials and how to deliver the National Curriculum to younger students.
    c *Geography* is written for teachers and students studying post-16 geography. It is an invaluable source of up-to-date case study material.
○ Access to the 'Why Argue' project, which looks at the work in selected schools on how to liaise effectively with English and science teachers to ensure a coordinated approach to cross-curricular work.
○ Probably the most useful part of the site is the 'resources' section. You will be impressed by the search facility, which enables you to find free resources about a wide range of topics and themes. An example illustrates this. When 'education for sustainable development' was entered as the search term, the result was access to a wealth of free resources on this rapidly evolving and hugely important issue. Given that new examination board specifications promote this topic to a much greater degree, as a teacher you will need all the help you can get. In addition to this, take advantage of:

THE GEOGRAPHICAL ASSOCIATION'S WEBSITE

a The Countryside Commission's CD-ROM, posters and activities booklet.
b Friends of the Earth's 'Shout about Climate Change' pack. Materials for teachers in Key Stage 3 including teaching ideas, activities and lesson plans.
c Details relating to a visit to southern India. Teachers of primary and secondary geography have the opportunity to experience life in rural India and investigate local environmental projects.

There will be numerous occasions when you will want individuals or groups to search for information on the Internet as part of their research into a given topic. The IT department will probably have guidance notes about how to carry out an effective search. However, don't take it for granted that your students will transfer this knowledge and advice to your geography lesson.

Using the example of 'Hurricane Emily', one of the hurricanes to hit the Gulf of Mexico in early 2005, the value of advanced preparation and tighter search guidance can be illustrated. Typing Hurricane Emily into a Google search would give 3,370,000 hits – taxing for even the most experienced researcher, but nevertheless interesting if you want to read about the lives of a multitude of Emilys around the world!

A more refined and appropriate search is achieved by the use of quotation marks – "Hurricane Emily". Still 257,000 hits, but all directly relevant to the 2005 event.

Assuming you want to focus the research even further, recommend the use of more considered search words. Keying in "the track of Hurricane Emily" will reveal just 113 hits, all devoted to maps showing the movement of the hurricane.

Keying in "strength of Hurricane Emily" will give you just 58 hits, but they will all refer to the power of the hurricane in the context of the four categories of hurricane strength.

Enjoy more fruitful searching!

MORE EFFECTIVE SEARCHING ON THE INTERNET

MAKING USE OF YOUR SCHOOL'S INTRANET

As intranets evolve in schools, geography departments are set to maximize their use and their application to students' learning. You will need to work closely with your IT support team or your LEA adviser, but hard work and a visionary approach at the outset will pay huge dividends in the way you structure your teaching and the way your geography students structure their own learning.

At its simplest, an intranet is an internal, fully controlled version of the Internet. Students have rapid access to essential geographical information, avoiding unnecessary and sometimes distracting searches. As a teacher, you have the confidence that the materials they are working with are regulated and appropriate to the task in hand.

Set up a logical interface, to ease access. Be very selective as to what resources you want to include. Resources might include direct links to predetermined websites, a bank of images, diagrams, worksheets, writing frames, animations, video and sound clips, PowerPoint presentations, virtual field trips, GIS simulations, etc. The potential is endless. The ability to post exemplar, annotated students' work enhances assessment for learning and can be very motivating for individual students. The geography department can build administration and assessment systems into its intranet.

As school computer systems develop, it is becoming possible to access intranet materials from home. The potential for homework tasks and showcasing students' work is tremendous.

The aim of this idea is to encourage more geography teachers to find out about interactive whiteboards (IWBs), which are a wonderful aid to teaching and learning. If after reading this idea you are tempted to find out more, seek help from the experts. Your school's ICT department will help, or the LEA's ICT adviser. As stated in Idea 79, the Becta website is a great starting point, or indeed any of the specialist geography websites such as the Geographical Association's site (see Idea 83). Here you will get advice about:

o using IWBs to enhance teaching and learning strategies;
o the best packages to purchase;
o in-service training opportunities specifically for geography teachers;
o outstanding software.

So what do IWBs do? How could they enhance your teaching? Here is just a taste:

o Animations can show that geographical features are dynamic (e.g. volcanoes, urban patterns).
o Virtual field trips can be viewed or even created.
o Sound and video clips can be attached to worksheets.
o The IWB can be used to view live video links (weather satellites, live news reports, etc.).
o Interactive slideshows can be created. The teacher supplies the image, students annotate the image and save the outcomes.
o Scanned images from students' work or any published material can be projected, with sequenced annotation prepared in advance.
o Use the IWB to display the vast range of outstanding CD-ROMs available to geographers (see Idea 88).

USING INTERACTIVE WHITEBOARDS

Geographical information systems (GIS) have become one of the most powerful tools used by professionals who need to gain access to geographical information, to allow them to make decisions and solve problems. Given the huge potential of GIS, we need to develop our teaching programmes to ensure that students have the opportunity to use and apply GIS in a range of geographical contexts. There are many commercial products available for your use. They have been designed for use with the full age and ability range. Many CD-ROMs (see Idea 88) include GIS applications.

Essentially, GIS software enables users to collect information, store it, process it and then display outcomes in relation to places on a map or on an image of an area. If this sounds complicated and you are worried about how to introduce GIS into your lessons, don't worry! The Ordnance Survey website provides you with an outstanding package which is easy to navigate, well written and well presented, and it's free! The information and the simulation exercises are also supported by free downloadable factsheets and worksheets.

Students will enjoy learning about the practical application of GIS through contexts such as:

o optimizing the location of wind farms;
o making planning applications in urban areas;
o establishing optimum delivery routes for home-delivered shopping.

Students are then challenged to a range of GIS missions where simulations require them to apply GIS to issues such as:

o flood damage control;
o crime hotspots;
o farm management.

There are probably more CD-ROMs available for geography than for any other subject. If you have never sampled them, you are missing out on a fabulous resource. Research on teaching and learning proves beyond all doubt that, with careful use, CD-ROMs engage and motivate students of all ages and abilities. Used in conjunction with a PC or laptop and projector, CD-ROMs provide geography teachers with a wealth of resources and activities, e.g. image banks, worksheets, video and sound clips, animations, charts and statistics, differentiated assessments, games and simulations, etc. Task-related activities are a common feature. More recent CD-ROMs have recognized the need to differentiate tasks and materials. Writing frames are provided, and many activities are interactive for whole-class or individual use.

They are available from many sources. Commercial publishers have an increasing and extensive catalogue of CD-ROMs, covering every geographical topic from tourism through to river landforms and on to development issues in Brazil. In addition, you can purchase CD-ROMs from dedicated commercial organizations such as the Ordnance Survey (interactive atlas of the United Kingdom) or from charities such as Action Aid (development issues). The United Nations has invaluable CD-ROM material on topics such as measuring and analysing human development, and coping with physical and human disasters. Through gateways such as 'curriculum online' and Becta, you can obtain CD-ROMs written specifically to cover QCA schemes of work across the key stages. Exemplars of students working at different levels are available to illustrate learning opportunities and standards achieved.

DIGITAL CAMERAS

The increasing affordability and reduction in size of digital cameras has made them one of the great tools for use in a geography department. While the old saying 'you get what you pay for' is true, the images achieved with even the cheapest of cameras are sufficiently good to be useful to teachers and students of geography. It is useful to purchase a larger-capacity picture card than the standard one normally issued.

The best departments have a high-quality, multi-featured camera for use by geography staff; a number of cheaper, easier-to-use, reduced-feature cameras can be made available to students. Naturally, it is advisable to check out insurance details relating to the use of cameras by staff and students. The value of allowing students to use the cameras cannot be overestimated.

o Image costs are negligible, and consequently students can take and experiment with many images.
o Subsequent editing allows for a more refined selection of useful images and/or editing of individual images through many of the software packages available.
o Exporting to work files is easy and effective. Groups of students can share the fruits of their fieldwork.
o Annotation to develop and draw out the geographical understanding is possible, either by individuals or by whole classes when projectors or interactive whiteboards are used.
o It is easy to place the images on to the intranet for use with different students in subsequent years.

PowerPoint allows geographers to introduce dramatic visual images and provide a framework to support the structure of a talk. You can emphasize key points and add interest and variety through animation and non-text data. With increasing competence in the creation of PowerPoint presentations, you will see the value of merging graphics, tables and charts, links to files on a network or to the Web, audio and video clips, and animations.

The following guidance is offered to beginners:

o Use a maximum of eight lines on each slide; don't make the slide too 'busy'
o Use font size 44 for your titles and font size 28 for your text.
o Use a sans serif font for clarity; Arial is particularly good.
o Highlight text using colour or italics, as underlining is hard to read.

Don't overuse PowerPoint in your lessons; it loses its wow factor. Use it to support your talk, not to direct every minute of it. Challenge the students by asking open questions while you reveal text or graphics, video links, etc.

Encourage students to use it when you require illustrated talks from them; you will be impressed by their level of competence.

There are many pre-prepared PowerPoint presentations for geographers. An Internet search based on "PowerPoint presentations for geographers" will give you a head start. Quality materials can also be found using "Curriculum Online".

USING MICROSOFT POWERPOINT

ACCESSING CENSUS DATA: THE UK CENSUS

Access to up-to-date census data has never been easier. With the information, students can gain a real sense of place; they can investigate changes over time; they can make comparisons within regions, within countries and globally. In using census data, research skills are developed; the ability to select and refine data is developed; and when combined with a spreadsheet, data can easily be represented graphically.

Given that Web addresses change frequently, this and the next idea will draw your attention to three excellent Internet sites by providing 'search' words. Encourage all your colleagues to look at the websites; even reluctant users will enjoy interrogating them and recognizing the potential for their teaching programmes. Experience shows that students' learning is optimized when two basic recommendations are followed:

o Show your students how to navigate through the sites by projecting the Web pages on to a screen.
o Never give students an 'open-ended' search task. Provide them with a purpose and a clear route of inquiry.

The UK census data can be accessed using the search words "UK census 2001". This is a very useful database for geography teachers. While navigating around the site and getting to the heart of some of the best information will take a little getting used to, the search is worth it. At the touch of your keyboard, you can do any of the following:

o You can access the National Profile, with information on population, the economy, the environment, travel, etc.
o Comparisons can be made between different regions of the United Kingdom.
o Within regions, and facilitated by the use of postcodes, neighbourhood profiles can be drawn up. Information relating to population, families, ethnicity, health and work is available.

- Comparisons can be made to investigate change compared to the 1991 census.
- Factsheets are available to summarize the 2001 census.
- Students can participate in quizzes and compare student-generated census material with that from other countries.

In addition to UK census data, two other sources worth viewing can be found using the following search words:

o "Geohive". This is a free-access website that offers a wealth of population and economic data. Easy to navigate, it will provide you with up-to-date statistics and graphs by country, by region, by areas within regions and globally. It is regularly updated and provides students and staff with links to many more sites of value.

After visiting the site, you will quickly see the value and the potential it brings to enhance the learning programme. As with the previous idea, you should avoid introducing your students to the site until you have devised a simple task sheet to focus and direct their interrogation.

o "Upmystreet" (all one word) is the second free-access site that I would recommend for viewing. The site has been developed to help people who are considering moving into a specified area. Using a postcode, students can explore the characteristics of any area in the United Kingdom. At the home page, click on "local area" to access descriptive information relating to schools, crime, transport, leisure opportunities and the characteristics of the people who live there. Most established areas are also supported by a bank of photographs.

Geographers will be quick to recognize the potential for comparative study between one area and another. The use of this website in conjunction with UK census data provides great potential for lesson planning.

VIDEO/DVDS

Videotapes and latterly DVDs have been an essential resource for geographers over many years. Their use is dramatically enhanced when the images are projected on to a large screen using a good-quality sound system; students are more readily engaged, particularly if subtitles are used. (See Idea 21 on listening frames.)

DVDs give greater flexibility and speed if you want to rewind, fast-forward and critically 'pause' images. As with all things, the quality of the equipment will ultimately determine the quality of recording and playback. Don't underestimate the value of the remote control. As a controlling tool, the remote control can be helpful (it enables unexpected pausing and/or sudden muting when you want to admonish a student or a class). It significantly helps if movement away from the television or video or DVD player is advantageous.

An up-to-date cataloguing system is essential if the department has a large bank of video and DVD materials. Ideally, these will be catalogued on a spreadsheet where the 'find' facility enables you to seek out the excellent video you used eight months previously.

One critical factor is the need to keep your stock of videos and DVDs up to date. Don't become complacent and continue to use videos recorded several years ago just because you know the material back to front and they offer students some graphic moving images as part of their learning programme. Be aware that they may contain outdated information. We teach a fast-moving subject.

Other key ideas

FUN AT THE END OF TERM: TRADITIONAL GAMES

At the end of term and as a reward for the students' hard work, why not treat them to an activity which starts and ends with fun? There are many activities that you can devise yourself from the standard quiz through to more ambitious activities such as playing simulation games such as the 'sugar plantation game' as recommended on the Qualifications and Curriculum Authority's 'innovating with geography'. Other activities quickly and easily developed by teachers or by the students themselves include:

o Hangman: this is ideal for reinforcing the use of technical words associated with a specific topic. For example, if the class knows that the overall theme is 'the water cycle', words to identify would include 'transpiration', 'throughflow', 'permeable', 'groundwater', etc.

o Local Monopoly: students have to create a Monopoly board based on their home area. The properties and road names have to reflect a knowledge and understanding of local street and area values, the utilities have to reflect local services, and the 'chance' and 'community chest' cards have to reflect local issues and events in terms of rewards or sanctions attached.

o Word searches: students have to design a word search on a given theme, e.g. ecosystem, or on things associated with a particular case study they have undertaken, e.g. Glasgow.

o Taboo: students have to explain or articulate a technical word without actually using the word, e.g. 'gentrification'. Their learning and the rest of the participants' learning is enhanced, while they have fun.

If devising your own end-of-term activities is too onerous and you have access to an IT suite (or interactive whiteboard), your problems are solved. There are a huge number of interactive geography games and simulations available to you. As always, it is advisable to test them out first, particularly if you want an entire class to access one particular site. Take time to explain the geography context and the reason why the activity has been selected to reinforce knowledge, understanding or skills. Remind the students that the activity is a reward for them, but they have a responsibility to remain on-task and not to stray into other, untried websites.

To recognize the huge variety of games available to you, search on geography+games+quizzes+simulations (no spaces). You will get over 8,000 hits. It is advisable to search UK sites only, as many of the US websites have quizzes and games embedded in the geography of the United States.

Within five minutes, I was able to access a wide variety of educational and fun activities, including:

o the Banana game (simulation and problem-solving activity);
o Geography Olympics (interactive game testing students' knowledge of location);
o Map Zone (great fun with Ordnance Survey maps);
o Match It (definitions against key words or phrases across every geography topic under the sun).

The list goes on and on!

KEEPING YOURSELF UP TO DATE

Earlier in this book, you were presented with good reasons why you should keep senior managers and parents up to date about what you are doing in geography. In the fast-moving world of education, geography continues to fight and elbow its way into a position of prominence. Not only have geographers got to position themselves within an increasingly competitive world, particularly with reference to the 14–19 phase of education, but they have to rise to the challenge of keeping up to date with the explosion of new ideas and resources available to them. One of the last tips in this book is to steer you towards the Qualifications and Curriculum Authority's Geography Update materials. Find this material with ease by going to the QCA website. The materials can be downloaded for free, for use within your department.

The information is clearly written, concise, very informative and well presented. The contributors know what they are talking about. To give you a flavour of what is available, look at the following topics. These appeared in the most recent update, produced as this book was being prepared.

o Embedding English in geography
o A new look to Key Stage 3
o Innovating with Geography website
o Pilot geography GCSE
o Geography monitoring work 2004/5
o Futures: meeting the challenge
o QCA/DfES geography websites and publications
o Embedding mathematics in geography
o QCA assessment project
o Using innovating with geography
o Introducing cultural geography
o Student choice 14–19
o 14–19 Education and Skills White Paper
o Useful website addresses

Challenge any of your colleagues and your A-level students with the task of naming all 25 member states of the European Union. The list below was accurate at the time of writing (it includes the new member states* as of 1 May 2004).

Austria	Belgium	Cyprus*	Czech Republic*
Denmark	Estonia*	Finland	France
Germany	Greece	Hungary*	Ireland
Italy	Latvia*	Lithuania*	Luxembourg
Malta*	Netherlands	Poland*	Portugal
Slovakia*	Slovenia*	Spain	Sweden
United Kingdom			

No doubt they will struggle with the task. They might be surprised that the number totals 25!

Geographers are expected to keep up to date with the fast-changing world that surrounds them. Moreover, they are expected to ensure that the resources used by students are accurate and current. It is essential that the geography department remains committed to reviewing its stock of basic texts. The atlas used in each classroom is one of the most important resources to keep under review.

o Is it Myanmar or Burma?
o Is it Mumbai or Bombay?
o Where is Moldova?
o How many sovereign states were created from the former Yugoslavia?
o Do the indicators of development (as listed in the back of most good atlases) reflect the rapid development of South Korea?

These questions illustrate the problem. If, through tight budgets, you have to use slightly dated materials, at least share the issue with your students. At least the problem illustrates how fast the world is changing!

TEACHING GIFTED AND
TALENTED GEOGRAPHERS

A small number of students in any key stage will exhibit special gifts and talents in their geographical studies. This idea suggests a number of strategies to ensure that you challenge and stimulate your most gifted students. Ensure that you work within the framework established by your school, as gifted students can exhibit talents in a wide range of areas. Unless your work is coordinated alongside others', the students can be overwhelmed by an enriched educational diet.

Don't take on too much in the first instance, as development work in this area can be very time-consuming. A good starting point is to identify one or two units in each key stage. Focus on these and create extension materials within the scheme of work. The extension materials could be:

o questions that require increasing intellectual ability to answer;
o resource materials that are increasingly sophisticated (in terms of readability, depth, perspective, etc.);
o tasks that require the student to find out more on his or her own initiative.

Another tactic is to broaden the learning experience in geography by planning extended activities and events, such as:

o a focused work experience programme, perhaps in a planning office or with organizations such as an environmental pressure group;
o allowing younger students to accompany sixth-form groups when they attend conferences or debates.

If these ideas provoke you into finding out more about the way you can enhance the learning programme for these students, help is at hand. The Qualifications and Curriculum Authority provides geography teachers with some really useful guidance and some very practical advice about what to do. Access this information through the National Curriculum website (www.nc.uk.net/gt /index.html). While generic advice is available, the website provides you with details directly relevant to geography, and exemplar material is provided to save you time in preparing new resources.

In the hectic world in which we work, forging links with feeder primary schools is often the last thing on our mind and on our agenda. In recognizing the multitude of other commitments to ensure quality geography delivery in our school, there is value in finding time to be mutually supportive. The first unit of geography in Key Stage 3 encourages you to make links with what students learned and understood while studying geography in their primary school. By building on local studies undertaken in Key Stage 2, the first challenge is to further develop inquiry skills and mapping skills (to name just two). Beyond this, students are asked to contrast their home area with the study of new, contrasting localities.

Aside from this prescribed curriculum link, consider the following:

○ developing geography resources and tasks that transfer with the students, headed with the feeder and receiving schools' names;
○ loaning expensive resources to primary colleagues such as class sets of local Ordnance Survey maps and aerial photographs;
○ carrying out mutual lesson observations across the key stages to reinforce knowledge of geography delivery and develop a better understanding of assessment;
○ extending gifted and talented students by asking them to develop a resource (a bank of digital pictures?) or factsheets aimed at younger students.

LINKS WITH PRIMARY SCHOOLS

Why not take inspiration from an exhibition at Tate Britain in 2005, 'A Picture of Britain' and the parallel BBC4 television programme *A Digital Picture of Britain*? Ask students to submit their own pictures from across the Britain Isles to create your own department's library of images showing Britain's urban, rural and industrial landscapes.

Set against a large wall map of the country, pictures can be displayed with basic details of each location. At a more sophisticated level, the same effect could be achieved on the school intranet. If the school curriculum includes a photography course (or an art applied photography course), you could liaise with the teaching team to ensure that advice is provided about taking the pictures and/or to obtain advice about improving the pictures through image enhancing.

A prize could be awarded on an annual basis for the best photograph submitted; you could break the prizes down into categories (people, the environment, urban landscapes, etc.). A further development could be to engage parents in the venture. Through the school newsletter, invite them to submit their own pictures and brief commentary. Display their contributions on an open evening or an information evening